HOT!

HOT!

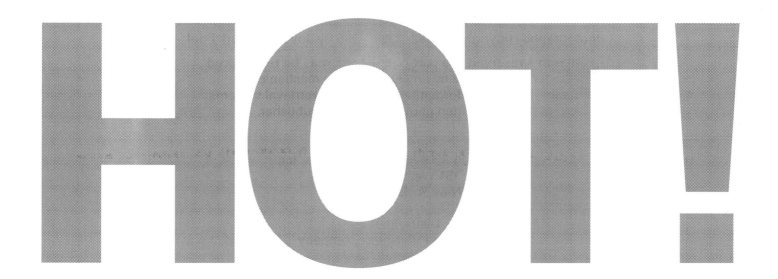

150 Fiery and Spicy Recipes
for cooking with chilies, peppercorns, mustard, horseradish, and ginger

Janet Hazen
Photography by Joyce Oudkerk Pool

BLACK DOG
& LEVENTHAL
PUBLISHERS

Published by
Black Dog & Leventhal Publishers, Inc.
151 West 19th Street
New York, NY 10011

Distributed by
Workman Publishing Company
708 Broadway
New York, NY 10003

Manufactured in Singapore

ISBN:1-884822-96-7

h g f e d c b a

Library of Congress Cataloging-in-Publication Data

Hazen, Janet.
Hot!:150 fiery and spicy recipes for cooking with
chilies, peppercorns, mustard, horseradish, and ginger
Janet Hazen; photography by Joyce Oudkerk Pool.
    p. cm.
Includes index.
ISBN 1-884822-96-7
1.Cookery, International. 2.Spices. I. Title.
TX725.A1H353   1997
641.59—dc21   97-22641
                                         CIP

TABLE OF
CONTENTS

RECITES

$\mathscr{I}$NTRODUCTION

CONSUMING SIZZLING-HOT, SPICY FOODS INDUCES TONGUE-SEARING, SINUS-CLEARING, throat-stinging, and chest-warming sensations that seduce and intoxicate. Once bitten by the fiery food bug, most devotees launch a never-ending search for ingredients guaranteed to generate that unmistakable high. They are enthralled with foods that flame the palate, bring tears to the eyes and sweat to the brow.

The scientific or, some might say, psychological explanation for this phenomenon is related to the human response to that well-known thin line between pain and pleasure. The theory is that once your mouth has been set ablaze, the brain releases endorphins, which produce a morphine-like reaction in the body (athletes, especially long-distance runners, also experience this reaction when exercising). Hence, the expression "It hurts so bad it feels good" holds true even in the gustatory realm.

The hot food craze has hit nearly every faction of our culinary world. Stories about torrid ingredients are featured on the front pages of newspaper food sections nationwide. Magazine articles on the subject appear on a regular basis, and there is at least one publication devoted solely to the topic of chili peppers. Restaurant diners are fearlessly experimenting with the incendiary dishes featured on Chinese, Thai, Vietnamese, Indian, and African menus. Home cooks now have the option of purchasing a wide range of fiery ingredients through mail-order catalogs and from stores that feature combustible comestibles from all over the world.

Fresh and dried chili peppers, the most popular source of culinary fire, still hold first place in terms of available firepower and their effect on the palate. Not to be overlooked, however, are such heat-lending ingredients as horseradish, mustard, peppercorns, and fresh ginger root.

Palate-awakening and blood-stimulating fresh horseradish root clears the head while providing a blast to the tongue. Until recently, this pungent condiment was primarily reserved as an accompaniment to roast beef and prime rib and for mixing with sour cream to serve with baked potatoes. Contemporary cooks, however, are finding broader culinary applications for the distinctively flavored root. More and more we see both fresh horseradish root and prepared horseradish paired with smoked and fresh fish, poultry, and meat dishes and in vegetable, grain, and potato salads.

Sparkling fresh, earthy, and pointed in flavor, fresh ginger root warms the mouth gently when cooked; raw it supplies a decided bite. Whether cooked or raw, pickled, candied, or preserved in brine, ginger has been a staple of most Asian kitchens for centuries. Dried and ground to a powder, American and European cooks have included powdered ginger in baked goods, in hot, spiced beverages, and even in ales and beer. In this book, the refreshing flavor of ginger adds a pleasant bite to a broad range of recipes.

Most people's familiarity with peppercorns is limited to the black pepper that sits atop the dining table in a miserable preground state, loaded with fillers and already stale when purchased. Black pepper is largely taken for granted, and most average kitchens do not contain white pepper, much less green or pink peppercorns. If you have yet to discover the virtues of cooking and seasoning with freshly ground peppercorns, whether black, white, green, or pink, then perhaps this book will serve as inspiration.

As of late, prepared mustards have taken the condiment spotlight, and it's about time. Regretably, many people have long ignored the exciting culinary potential of mustard. Until recently, the few conventional uses for mustard included smearing it on bread when making ham and cheese sandwiches, lining the top of a hot dog at baseball games, and occasionally adding it to cream sauces. Luckily, with so many delicious mustards on the market, the average consumer has moved away from these rather predictable and mundane uses and has embraced mustard as an indispensable condiment and cooking ingredient.

The recipes in this book are rated on a scale of 1 to 10, with 10 the hottest rating. There is a great deal of subjectivity in this area, however. Among five people, one food can provoke a different reaction in each. Generally speaking, we have similar tolerances for the temperature of food, but sensitivity to salty, sweet, pungent, and spicy qualities varies from one individual to the next. Therefore, the ratings applied to recipes in this collection may not correspond precisely to your particular palate. For this reason it's wise to view the ratings only as a general guideline.

Dedicated hotheads will find many delicious ways to walk the line between pleasure and pain within the chapters of this book, and the uninitiated may well become converts. A few dishes generate enough heat to earn the highest rating, others produce only a mild warming sensation, but all contain robustly flavored ingredients with distinctive character. Cook up some of these dishes and indulge in a meal saturated with invigorating flavors, fresh ingredients, healthful components, and seductive, fiery intensity.

FROM SOUP TO NUTS

STOCKING YOUR PANTRY: In addition to the flavor arsenal provided by chilies, ginger, horseradish, mustard, and peppercorns, which are discussed in the chapter introductions, there are a few commercially prepared items I find vital to vegetarian cookery. Chinese mushroom soy sauce, Japanese miso, and Italian or domestic dried mushrooms can be used to add intense flavor and body to soups, stews, sauces, dressings, and sautéed dishes. They can heighten the taste of most any dish without adding fat; their bold characteristics help take the place of meat or poultry in a vegetarian dish.

To provide flexibility in creating new dishes and to make many of the recipes in this book, you will find it very useful to have the following ingredients on hand: regular soy sauce (some folks also use tamari sauce); black and regular rice wine vinegar; balsamic, red wine, and champagne or white wine vinegars; peanut, vegetable, and olive oils; canned tomatoes, tomato paste in a tube, and sun-dried tomatoes; an assortment of dried and canned beans; a variety of grains such as cracked wheat, cornmeal, barley, buckwheat, and jasmine and wild rice; and several different kinds of dried pasta.

In my refrigerator I also try to stock jars of Chinese hot black bean, chili, hoisin, and plum sauces; a variety of domestic and imported olives; assorted nuts and nut butters; imported Parmesan cheese (chunk form—not pregrated); and Asian sesame oil. Armed with these staples, you can make a nutritious and flavor-packed grain or pasta dish in just minutes. You won't have any excuse for bland or boring dishes coming from your kitchen with a battery of such potent-tasting condiments. Even prepared foods can be doctored to a palatable state using one or two of these ingredients.

TAKING STOCK: For vegetarian cookery, one of the most important staples to have on hand is good-quality vegetable stock, for which I have included a basic recipe (following). You can use it to make soups and stews; to make sauces or dressings; to add to sautéed vegetables; or for cooking grains. When you make a pot of homemade vegetable stock, you may want to double the recipe so that you can freeze some for later use. You'll find it very convenient to have varying sizes of containers of the frozen stock in your freezer to thaw as needed for cooking.

If you're pressed for time, a good alternative is canned vegetable broth, a marvelous new product. Although both regular and low-sodium varieties contain hefty doses of sodium compared to homemade stock, they are an invaluable time-saver for last-minute cooking.

vegetable stock

➤ Use the basic stock that follows in recipes that call for homemade vegetable stock. I have suggested ingredients based on seasonal vegetables, but you can experiment with a variety of fresh or slightly wilted vegetables, depending on what you have in your refrigerator. Avoid using eggplant, potatoes, and large amounts of celery leaves and bell peppers, however, as these ingredients can make the stock bitter and give it an "off" taste.

Although the two ingredient lists ("Fall and Winter"; "Spring and Summer") allow the cook to take advantage of seasonal vegetables to prepare stock, either list produces a rich-tasting, full-bodied vegetable stock suitable for use in any of the recipes in this book.

makes about 4 quarts

Place the vegetables (and peppercorns, for Fall and Winter Stock) in a 12-quart, heavy-bottomed pot and sweat over high heat 3 to 4 minutes, stirring frequently, until they are warm and aromatic. Add 6 quarts of the water and bring to a boil. Reduce the heat to moderate and simmer 2 hours, stirring occasionally. Add the remaining water and cook 1½ hours. Strain through a colander and discard the solids. Strain a second time through a fine wire sieve. Cool to room temperature. Transfer to a container with a tight-fitting lid and store in the refrigerator for up to 4 days or in smaller containers in the freezer for up to 3 months.

FALL AND WINTER VEGETABLE STOCK:

3 large onions, coarsely chopped

½ small winter squash, coarsely chopped

4 medium carrots, coarsely chopped

4 stalks celery, coarsely chopped

16 mushrooms, quartered

3 medium zucchini, coarsely chopped

½ pound green beans, coarsely chopped

2 large tomatoes, coarsely chopped

1 head garlic, smashed

1½ tablespoons black peppercorns

9 quarts cold water

SPRING AND SUMMER VEGETABLE STOCK:

2 large onions, coarsely chopped

3 bunches scallions, coarsely chopped

2 medium carrots, coarsely chopped

2 stalks celery, coarsely chopped

3 medium zucchini, coarsely chopped

2 ears corn, cut into five sections

2 large tomatoes, coarsely chopped

½ pound green beans, coarsely chopped

½ pound asparagus, coarsely chopped

½ pound snow or sugar snap peas, coarsely chopped

6 cloves garlic

9 quarts cold water

chilies

$\mathscr{C}$ HILIES

IN THE KINGDOM OF BLISTERING, SCORCHING-HOT FOODS, IT IS THE MIGHTY CHILI PEPPER THAT wears the crown. Whether yellow, orange, red, green, or deep violet in color, fresh and dried chili peppers—the fruit of species of the Capsicum genus—are universally popular in the world of incendiary foods.

Historical evidence suggests that chili peppers were a common cooking ingredient as early as 4000 B.C. The Aztecs and Mayans in Central and South America and Indians in the West Indies had used fresh chilies for centuries, but it wasn't until after Columbus's second journey to these regions in 1495 that chili peppers were introduced to the Old World. The Spanish returned home with the plant, where it thrived in the hot, sunny climate of the Mediterranean. Portuguese and Spanish traders spread the chili pepper on their travels to Africa, India, and the Far East, where they were quickly assimilated into the native cuisines. By the 1600s chili peppers had been introduced to virtually every region of the world.

Native to South America, chili peppers are now cultivated in India, Mexico, China, Indonesia, Thailand, and the United States—where New Mexico, Texas, California, Arizona, and Louisiana are the leading growers. Typically, chilies grow best in hot, humid climates with long growing seasons, but many varieties also do well in mild, temperate zones.

Flamboyant, assertive, and visually appealing, chili peppers can be mild and sweet, warm and complex, or painfully hot. It is difficult to differentiate and classify the hundreds of varieties; deviations within individual classes make it even harder to predict the level of heat contained within a given chili pepper. Since the capsaicin, contained primarily in the veins and seeds, is the element in chilies that dictates overall heat level, one way to determine the fire potential of a chili is by counting its veins and examining the quantity of seeds. Generally speaking, fruits with a higher ratio of veins and seeds to flesh are hotter than those with proportionately fewer veins and seeds. Additionally, those grown in hotter climates tend to be a bit more fiery. Even within the same variety there can be a range of intensities; a jalapeño grown in one area may differ greatly from another grown only two miles away.

In 1902, pharmacologist Wilber Scoville developed a method for measuring the amount, or power, of capsaicin in a given pepper. Originally, Scoville presented tasters with a mixture of ground chilies, sugar, alcohol, and water. Values were given according to the amount of diluting ingredients (sugar, alcohol, and water) necessary to make the mixture devoid of heat. Today computers perform this challenging task, rating peppers by Scoville Units, which indicate parts per million of capsaicin.

Next time you bite into a sizzling speck of edible fire and it happens to be a jalapeño chili pepper, remember this: The Scoville scale begins at zero with mild bell peppers, and moves into the lower mid-range, with the cascabel rating four (out of ten) and a unit measurement of 1,500 to 2,500. Relatively innocuous jalapeños rank dead center with a unit rating of 2,500 to 5,000. Cayenne, tabasco, aji, and piquin peppers, packed with approximately 30,000 to 50,000 Scoville Units, rank number eight out of ten. The scale tops off with the wicked and much-prized habanero and Bahamian chilies, which contain between 100,000 and 300,000 Scoville Units. In comparison, that minuscule little grain of jalapeño that seared your mouth is relatively benign.

With over four hundred varieties being grown today, the availability and assortment of fresh and dried chili peppers is staggering. If you cannot find the exact type of pepper called for in the following recipes, substitute one of similar size, color, and approximate heat intensity.

When purchasing fresh chili peppers, look for fruit that is firm, smooth, free of blemishes, and even colored. Store fresh chilies in a plastic bag in the refrigerator for up to two weeks. If your purchases begin to show signs of age and you have no immediate use for them, roast, peel, seed, and stem the chilies and either store in the freezer in a tightly sealed container for up to six to eight months, or cover with peanut or olive oil and store in a tightly sealed container in the refrigerator for up to two months. Alternatively, you can "pickle" the roasted peppers by covering them with a mild vinegar, or marinate them with a mixture of oil and vinegar and perhaps some garlic and herbs.

Dried peppers ought to be glossy and free of holes, tears, and insects (some prepackaged dried chili peppers imported from Mexico come with unexpected extras—tiny flying bugs).

Store dried chili peppers in tightly sealed plastic or paper bags in a cool, dark place for up to one year; six months is optimal. To rehydrate, place the chilies in a bowl and cover with hot or warm water (top with a smaller bowl filled with water to keep them submerged). Soak at room temperature until soft and pliable. Depending on the type of chili, this could take as little as fifteen minutes or as long as three hours. Generally speaking, the hotter the soaking liquid the faster the pepper rehydrates. However, some feel that boiling hot water brings out a bitter taste in dried chili peppers; I have yet to find this to be true.

Despite their reputation, not all dishes containing chili peppers are exceedingly torrid. Certainly not all of the recipes that follow will scorch your mouth, but a few potential palate-burners, such as *Ethiopian Onion-and Ginger-Stuffed Jalapeños* or *Chilled Tomato-Shrimp Bisque with Ancho and Chipotle Chilies,* could bring a tear to your eye.

Sensitive palates will appreciate the flavor-packed *Burmese Beef and Potato Coconut Curry* and the *Doro Wat* (Ethiopian chicken stew), two rich, satisfying dishes that improve with age up to three or four days. Both can easily be made twice as hot by doubling the amount of chili peppers. However, more is not necessarily better with all the recipes. Increasing the number of peppers called for in the *Shrimp and Melon Salad with Cayenne-Serrano Vinaigrette* or in the *Chocolate-Coffee Brownies with Chipotle Chilies* would destroy their delicate flavor balance by allowing one taste and one sensation to dominate. We all like to set our heads afire from time to time, but not every dish is designed to deliver a dose of capsaicin powerful enough to peel paint.

Two CAUTIONARY NOTES: When preparing fresh and dried chili peppers, either wear gloves or refrain from touching any mucus membranes until you're certain your hands are free from the natural oils. Even repeated hand washing with hot water and soap will not fully remove the capsaicin-containing oils. Secondly, if you happen to get in over your head during a typical hothead dining experience, and you suddenly find your mouth going into orbit, *do not drink water!* Consumption of water only intensifies the agonizing burning sensation. Instead, drink milk or eat some yogurt—even buttered bread, tortillas, or rice can help.

roasted chili pepper nuts

10 ounces macadamia nuts

8 ounces pistachio nuts

8 ounces almonds

8 ounces pumpkin seeds

4 ancho chili peppers

4 dried cayenne or chiltepe chili peppers

3 dried cascabel chili peppers

2 dried guajillo or New Mexico chili peppers

1 chipotle chili pepper

1½ tablespoons Hungarian paprika

2 tablespoons kosher salt, or to taste

1½ tablespoons ground cumin

3 tablespoons olive oil

2 tablespoons unsalted butter, melted

➤ Serve these spiced nuts as hors d'oeuvres or snacks with cocktails, beer, or soft drinks. Finely chopped, they make a great topping for casserole dishes, sautéed mixed vegetables, or tossed green salads.

This particular combination of nuts forms a balanced, well-rounded blend of flavors, but feel free to substitute your favorite nuts for one or two of the types specified in the recipe.

HOTTER 5

makes about 3½ cups

Preheat oven to 325° F. Place nuts and pumpkin seeds in a large mixing bowl. Set aside.

Arrange the ancho, cayenne, cascabel, guajillo, and chipotle chili peppers on a baking sheet. Roast 3 to 5 minutes or until aromatic, puffy, and a shade darker. Remove from the oven and cool to room temperature. Remove stems and seeds and discard. Using an electric spice grinder, pulverize the chilies in batches to a fine powder. Add to the nuts along with the paprika, salt, and cumin; mix well. Drizzle the oil and butter over the nuts and mix well.

Divide the nuts between two baking sheets, making a single layer on each. Bake in the oven 25 to 27 minutes, rotating pans between shelves and stirring the nuts from time to time. Remove from the oven and cool to room temperature. Serve immediately or store in tightly sealed plastic bags in the refrigerator for up to 3 weeks. Bring to room temperature before serving.

Chili Shrimp Corn Cakes
with Chipotle Mayonnaise

Chipotle Mayonnaise:

2 egg yolks

2 cloves garlic, minced

⅓ cup vegetable oil

⅓ cup olive oil

2 tablespoons fresh lime juice

1½ tablespoons minced chipotle peppers (see Note)

Salt and pepper, to taste

Chili Shrimp Corn Cakes:

3 dried ancho or pasilla chilies

¾ pound small prawns

2 jalapeño peppers, seeded, stemmed, and minced

1 tablespoon ground coriander

1½ cups fresh corn kernels (about 2 ears of corn)

These golden brown shrimp and corn cakes are made with fresh and dried chilies and are served with a fiery mayonnaise made with smoked and dried jalapeños called chipotle peppers. Find these dried chili peppers in bulk in natural food stores or in Latin markets. They are also sold canned in adobo sauce. I prefer to buy them in the sauce as they have extra flavor and are already reconstituted.
Makes 4 to 6 servings (12 cakes)   *Hotter: rated 5*

To make the Chipotle Mayonnaise: Place the egg yolks and garlic in a small bowl. Slowly add the vegetable oil, drop by drop, incorporating it all the while with a wire whisk to form a smooth emulsion. When all the vegetable oil has been added, slowly add the olive oil in a thin stream, whisking all the while. Add the lime juice and chipotle pepper: mix well. Season with salt and pepper and store in the refrigerator, covered, until needed.

To make the Chili Shrimp Corn Cakes: Soak the dried chilies in boiling water to cover for 2 to 3 hours or until soft and pliable. Remove the seeds and stems, and mince. Place in a large bowl and set aside until needed.

Bring a large pot of water to a boil over high heat. Add the prawns and cook for 1 minute. Remove, drain, and rinse with cold water. When the prawns are cool enough to handle, remove shells and tails. Finely chop and add to the chilies.

Cook the jalapeño pepper, coriander, and corn in the olive oil over moderate heat for 5 minutes, stirring frequently. Add the green onions and cilantro and cook for 2 minutes over high heat, stirring constantly. Remove from the pan and add to the prawns and chilies; mix well and cool to room temperature. Add the sour cream, eggs, and ½ cup of the bread crumbs; mix well and season with salt and pepper. Refrigerate, covered, for 2 hours or up to 1 day.

Remove the corn cake mixture from the refrigerator. Using about 1½ tablespoons at a time, form into 12 patties. Coat all sides with bread crumbs and refrigerate for 1 hour.

Heat ½ inch of vegetable oil in a very large, nonstick sauté pan over moderately high heat. When the oil is hot, add a batch of the cakes and cook until golden brown on the first side, about 1 minute. Carefully flip, using a rubber spatula, and cook the second side until golden brown. Drain on paper towels and serve immediately with sprigs of cilantro and Chipotle Mayonnaise.

Note: If your chipotle peppers are dried rather than canned, soak them for 2 to 3 hours in warm water to cover until soft and pliable, and stem, seed, and mince them before proceeding.

3 tablespoons olive oil

1 small bunch green onions, minced

½ cup chopped cilantro leaves

¾ cup sour cream

2 eggs, lightly beaten

1½ cups fine dried bread crumbs

Salt and pepper, to taste

Vegetable oil, for cooking

Cilantro sprigs, for garnish

Watermelon-Jicama Salad
with Jalapeños

Jalapeño Syrup:

½ **cup fresh lime juice**

½ **cup water**

½ **cup sugar**

**6 jalapeño peppers, stemmed
and cut in thin rounds**

**2 cups seeded and cubed
watermelon**

**1 small jicama, peeled and
cut in julienne (1½ to 2 cups)**

Mint sprigs, for garnish

This refreshing summer salad is simple and easy to prepare, and makes an out-standing appetizer or side dish to serve with grilled poultry or fish. Grilled prawns mixed into this combination would also be delicious.
Makes 4 servings.   *Hotter: rated 6*

To make the Jalapeño Syrup: Combine the lime juice, water, and sugar in a small saucepan. Bring to a boil over moderate heat. Boil for 10 to 15 minutes, until the mixture is thick and syrupy. Add the jalapeño pepper and cook for 5 minutes. Remove from the heat and cool to room temperature.

Arrange the watermelon and jicama on a plate. Drizzle the jalapeño syrup over the fruit, topping with the jalapeño rounds. Garnish with fresh mint, and serve slightly chilled or at cool room temperature.

Thai Squid Salad with Three Chilies

Dressing:

¼ cup peanut oil

2 tablespoons *nuoc cham* (fish sauce)

2 tablespoons fresh lime juice

Zest from 2 limes

3 cloves garlic, thinly sliced

2 jalapeño peppers or serrano chilies, cut in thin rounds

Salt and pepper, to taste

2 tablespooons peanut oil

3 cups cleaned squid bodies, cut into ½-inch rings, and tentacles (about 3 pounds whole squid bodies)

1 small red onion, halved and thinly sliced

1 red bell pepper, cut in julienne

3 jalapeño peppers, stemmed and cut in thin rounds

8 or more butter lettuce leaves

½ cup mint leaves

½ cup cilantro leaves

2 tablespoons dried red pepper flakes

½ cup roasted peanuts, coarsely chopped

This classic Thai salad is perfect for those on a low-fat, low-calorie diet. If squid is difficult to find, use small- or medium-sized prawns instead (remove shells and tails and cook in the peanut oil for 2 to 2½ minutes). This salad is at once hot and fiery, refreshing and invigorating.
Makes 4 to 6 servings.   *Hottest: rated 8*

To make the dressing: Place the peanut oil in a small bowl. Use a wire whisk to incorporate the fish sauce a little at a time, whisking all the while. Add the lime juice and the zest, garlic, and jalapeño peppers: mix well. Set aside at room temperature until needed.

Heat the oil in a large skillet over high heat. When the oil is hot, add the squid and cook, stirring constantly, for 1 to 1½ minutes or until the squid is just done. Do not overcook the squid or it will be tough and rubbery.

Place the squid in a large bowl along with the red onion, bell pepper, jalapeño pepper, and the dressing; mix well. Arrange on the lettuce leaves, and garnish with the mint, cilantro, red pepper flakes, and peanuts. Serve immediately.

Shrimp and Melon Salad with Cayenne-Serrano Vinaigrette

COOL, REFRESHING HONEYDEW MELON AND SUCCULENT PRAWNS FORM A SWEET-SAVORY BACKDROP FOR THIS SALAD'S SIZZLING-HOT VINAIGRETTE. THE COMBINATION OF RED AND GREEN HOT CHILI PEPPERS MAKES FOR A VERY STRIKING SALAD.

MAKES 4 SERVINGS. ∼ **HOTTEST #7**

CAYENNE-SERRANO VINAIGRETTE:

½ cup peanut oil

2 tablespoons each fresh orange and lemon juice

1 teaspoon cayenne pepper

4 serrano chili peppers, stemmed, halved, seeded, and thinly sliced

Salt and pepper, to taste

SHRIMP AND MELON SALAD:

1 pound large prawns

1 small honeydew melon, cut into eighths, peeled, seeded, and cut into ⅛-inch-wide slices

⅓ cup finely chopped fresh mint leaves

TO MAKE THE CAYENNE-SERRANO VINAIGRETTE: Place the peanut oil in a small bowl. Slowly add the orange and lemon juices, whisking constantly with a wire whisk to form a smooth emulsion. Add the cayenne pepper and serrano chilies and mix well. Season with salt and pepper and set aside until needed.

Bring 3 quarts of water to boil in a 5-quart saucepan. Add the prawns and cook 1 to 1½ minutes, just until the prawns are opaque in the center. Take care not to overcook the prawns. Drain in a colander and refresh with cold water. Cool to room temperature. When cool enough to handle, remove the shells and tails and discard.

Arrange the melon and prawns on a large plate. Drizzle with the vinaigrette and garnish with the mint. Serve at cool room temperature.

Ethiopian Onion- and Ginger-Stuffed Jalapeños

This is my rendition of a traditional dish described to me by an Ethiopian friend. Not for the faint of heart, it is made with fierce jalapeño chilies stuffed with a piquant, fiery, ginger-accented filling. This is the quintessential appetizer for hotheads.

Makes 8 to 12 servings. ⌒ **Hottest #10**

In a 3-quart saucepan, bring 2 quarts of salted water to boil over high heat. Add the jalapeño peppers and cook 1 minute. Drain in a colander, refresh with cold water, and immediately transfer to a bowl filled with ice water. When the chili peppers are thoroughly chilled, drain in a colander and pat dry with a clean kitchen towel.

Using a sharp paring knife, on each chili make a ½-inch-long incision across the pepper, just under the stem. Starting at the right side of the incision, cut lengthwise along the pepper, making one side of a V-shaped cut, stopping approximately ¼ inch before the tip. Return to the left side of the cross-wise incision, make another V-shaped cut down to the bottom of the chili pepper, and remove the triangular piece of flesh. You should have a narrow, V-shaped opening. Carefully remove and discard the seeds, taking care not to tear the peppers. Set aside until needed.

In a large sauté pan, cook the onion and cumin in the butter over moderately high heat for 5 minutes, stirring frequently. Add the garlic and ginger and cook 2 to 3 minutes, stirring frequently. Season with salt and pepper and cool to room temperature. Dividing equally, gently stuff each jalapeño with the filling, taking care not to tear the flesh. Garnish with the serrano chilies and serve at room temperature.

12 large jalapeño chili peppers

1 medium onion, minced

1 teaspoon ground cumin

2 tablespoons unsalted butter

4 cloves garlic, minced

4-inch piece fresh ginger root, peeled and minced

Salt and pepper, to taste

3 red serrano chili peppers (or any other red chili pepper), stemmed, seeded, and minced, for garnish

Chinese Chicken Salad with Spicy Peanut Sauce

FRESH CHILI PEPPERS AND A GENEROUS DOSE OF PREPARED CHINESE HOT CHILI PASTE ADD FIRE AND SPARK TO THIS CLASSIC CHINESE CHICKEN SALAD. THE PEANUT SAUCE IS BEST IF PREPARED ONE TO TWO DAYS AHEAD.

MAKES ABOUT 6 SERVINGS. ⟩ HOTTEST #9

TO MAKE THE SPICY PEANUT SAUCE: In a medium bowl, combine the peanut butter, water, soy sauce, hoisin sauce, and vinegar, whisking with a wire whisk or fork to make a smooth emulsion. Add the sesame oil, garlic, ginger, serrano chilies, and chili paste; mix well. Season with salt and pepper, if desired. The sauce can be stored in a tightly sealed container in the refrigerator for up to 2 days. Bring to room temperature before serving.

Place the chicken breasts in a large pot and cover with cold water. Bring to a boil over high heat and cook 3 minutes. Remove from the heat and cover with a tight-fitting lid. Let stand at room temperature for at least 1 hour or up to 2 hours. Remove chicken from cooking liquid and cool to room temperature. When cool, remove the meat from the bones, taking care to separate the tendons and fat from the meat; discard all but the meat. Using your hands, shred the chicken into bite-size pieces.

Place the cabbage on a large platter and surround it with the cucumbers; top with the chicken. Spoon the sauce over the chicken and garnish with the cilantro and scallions. Serve at room temperature.

SPICY PEANUT SAUCE:

½ cup natural peanut butter

¼ cup water

4 tablespoons soy sauce

3 tablespoons hoisin sauce

2 tablespoons rice wine vinegar

1 tablespoon sesame oil

4 cloves garlic, minced

1½ tablespoons minced, peeled fresh ginger root

6 red serrano chili peppers, stemmed, seeded, and finely minced

2½ teaspoons Chinese hot chili paste

Salt and white pepper, to taste

3 large chicken breasts halves

4½ cups finely shredded white cabbage

½ English cucumber, peeled, halved lengthwise, and thinly sliced

¼ cup coarsely chopped fresh cilantro

⅓ cup finely chopped scallions

chili pepper–stuffed mushroom caps

21 large, very fresh mushrooms

2 tablespoons olive oil

2 tablespoons unsalted butter

2 cloves garlic, minced

2 bird's eye (Thai) chili peppers, stemmed and finely chopped

2 apple or small pimento chili peppers, stemmed, seeded, and finely chopped

2 hot goat horn or New Mexico chili peppers, stemmed, seeded, and finely chopped

1 Hungarian sweet chili pepper, stemmed, seeded, and finely chopped

1 1/2 teaspoons *each* dried thyme and sage

1/3 cup dry vermouth

1 1/3 cups finely ground dried bread crumbs

1 1/2 tablespoons sherry vinegar

Salt and pepper, to taste

➤ Hotheads and mushroom-lovers alike will enjoy this chili pepper–enhanced classic hors d'oeuvre.

Although they already pack a punch, for even more heat, use only bird's eye (Thai) chili peppers instead of the mixture suggested.

HOTTER 6
makes 18 mushrooms; 4 to 6 servings

Preheat oven to 400° F. Lightly grease a very shallow baking pan (a jelly roll pan is ideal).

Remove stems from 18 of the mushrooms and reserve caps. Finely chop the stems along with the 3 remaining mushrooms and set aside.

In a large sauté pan, heat the olive oil and butter over moderately high heat. Add the chopped mushrooms, garlic, chili peppers, and herbs. Increase the heat to high and cook 10 minutes, stirring frequently, until very soft and all the liquid has evaporated. Add the vermouth and cook 1 to 2 minutes, or until the liquid has almost evaporated. Add the bread crumbs and cook 3 minutes, stirring constantly, until lightly browned. Add the vinegar, salt, and pepper and mix well. Remove from the heat and cool to room temperature. (If the mixture seems too dry at this point you may add a little melted butter or olive oil.)

Tightly pack the cavity of each mushroom cap with the bread crumb mixture, rounding it into a dome shape. Place the mushrooms on the prepared pan, stuffed sides up, leaving approximately 3/4 inch between each one. Bake in the center of the oven 8 to 10 minutes, or until the mushrooms are tender and the filling is hot. Remove from the oven and serve immediately.

Cheese-Stuffed Peppers with Ancho Chili Sauce

This dish is made with mild sweet peppers filled with ground meat, rice, or both in eastern Europe; with temperate peppers in the Mediterranean; and with fiery chili peppers in Central and South America. The quintessential hot chili recipe, this one is for dedicated hotheads.
Makes 4 to 6 servings.   *Hottest: rated 10*

To make the Ancho Chili Sauce: Soak the dried chilies in 2 cups of boiling water for 4 to 6 hours, or until they are soft and pliable. Drain, reserving the soaking liquid. Stem and seed the chilies and coarsely chop. Set aside the chilies and the soaking liquid separately (and the puréed chipotle pepper, if used) until needed.

In a large saucepan, cook the onion, garlic, spices, and oregano in the olive oil over moderate heat for 10 minutes, stirring from time to time. Add the chilies and 2 cups of soaking liquid and bring to a boil over high heat. Reduce the heat to moderately high and cook for 15 minutes. Remove from the heat and cool slightly.

Purée the sauce in a blender and strain through a fine wire mesh. Return it to the saucepan, season with salt and pepper, and keep warm until needed. (Or the sauce can be refrigerated for up to 1 week.)

Preheat oven to 375° F.

Roast the fresh chilies until the skins just turn black. When cool enough to handle, carefully remove the skins, taking care not to break or tear the flesh of the chilies. Starting from the stem end, make a 1-inch slit in each chili. Gently remove the seeds and the interior portion of the stem; discard.

Combine the cheeses and cumin seed in a bowl; mix well. Carefully fill each pepper with the cheese mixture, once again taking care not to tear the chilies. Place the filled chilies in a lightly greased shallow baking dish and bake for 12 to 15 minutes or until the cheese is melted.

Remove chilies from the oven and serve on pools of the Ancho Chili Sauce. Garnish with a drizzle of Mexican crema, crème fraîche, or sour cream and sprigs of fresh oregano or cilantro.

Ancho Chili Sauce:

3 dried ancho chilies, coarsely chopped

3 dried poblano chilies, coarsely chopped

2 chipotle peppers (or 2 tablespoons puréed chipotle pepper)

2 cups boiling water

1 small red onion, coarsely chopped

3 cloves garlic, minced

1 teaspoon each ground mace, cinnamon, and oregano

¼ cup olive oil

Salt and pepper, to taste

6 large fresh poblano or California green chilies

½ pound Monterey Jack cheese, grated

¼ pound smoked Mozzarella or other natural smoked cheese, grated

¼ pound Asiago (or other hard grating cheese), grated

1 tablespoon cumin seed

Mexican crema, crème fraîche, or sour cream, for garnish

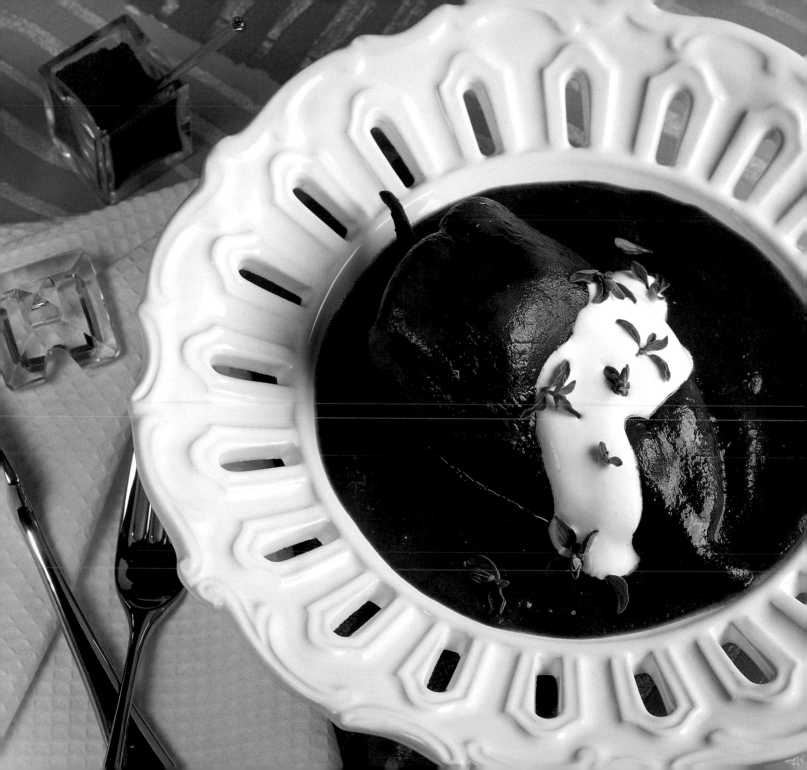

Roasted Red Pepper Soup with Green Chilies and Smoked Chicken

1 large onion, coarsely chopped

3 cloves garlic, minced

3 tablespoons ground cayenne pepper or small red chilies

1½ tablespoons ground coriander

1 teaspoon each ground mace, cloves, and cumin

3 tablespoons olive oil

3 tablespoons unsalted butter

2 quarts light chicken stock

4 large roasted red bell peppers, peeled, seeded, and coarsely chopped

3 roasted California or other long green chilies, seeded, stemmed, and sliced into thin strips

1 cup cubed or shredded smoked chicken or turkey meat

Salt and pepper, to taste

½ cup créme fraîche, for garnish

Sweet, mild red bell peppers combined with fiery dried chilies form the base of this beautiful red soup. The smokey taste of both the roasted peppers and the chicken make for a flavorful and unusual cold-weather dish. If you prefer a milder soup, reduce the amount of cayenne or small red chilies to 1½ tablespoons. Serve warm tortillas or tortilla chips and a green salad alongside.
Makes 6 to 8 servings.　　　　　　　　　　　　　*Hottest: rated 10*

In a large soup pot, cook the onion, garlic, and spices in the olive oil and butter over moderate heat for 10 minutes, stirring frequently. Add the chicken stock and red peppers and bring to a boil over high heat. Boil for 5 minutes, stirring frequently. Reduce the heat to moderate and cook for 15 minutes.

Cool the soup mixture to room temperature. Purée in a blender until smooth. Strain it through a fine wire mesh, and return it to the saucepan.

Bring the soup to a boil over high heat. Cook for 15 minutes over high heat, stirring frequently. Add all but a few strips of the roasted green chilies (chop the remaining chilies for garnish) and the chicken. Reduce heat to moderate and cook for 15 minutes. Season the soup with salt and pepper, and serve with a drizzle of crème fraîche and the chopped bits of the remaining green chilies.

Chilled Tomato-Shrimp Bisque with Ancho and Chipotle Chilies

I PREFER THE CONTRASTING EFFECT OF SPICY, PIQUANT FLAVORS COMBINED WITH A COLD SERVING TEMPERATURE IN
THIS SIMPLE-TO-PREPARE SOUP, BUT IF YOU'RE PRESSED FOR TIME, FEEL FREE TO SERVE IT IMMEDIATELY, PIPING HOT.
PAIR WITH A GREEN SALAD AND WARM BREAD FOR A COMPLETE MEAL.
MAKES ABOUT 6 SERVINGS. ∽ **HOTTEST #9**

1 large red onion, coarsely chopped

3 cloves garlic, coarsely chopped

4 red jalapeño chili peppers, stemmed, seeded,
and coarsely chopped

¼ cup olive oil

4 dried ancho chili peppers, stemmed and
coarsely chopped

4 dried chipotle chili peppers, stemmed and
coarsely chopped, or 2 tablespoons canned
chipotle chili peppers in adobo sauce, chopped

6 large tomatoes, cored and coarsely chopped

2 cups water

5 cups light chicken stock

1 cup heavy cream

Salt and pepper, to taste

1 pound small shrimp, peeled and
coarsely chopped

½ cup finely chopped fresh parsley

In a very large, heavy-bottomed pot, cook the onion, garlic, and jalapeño peppers in the olive oil over moderate heat for 5 minutes, stirring frequently. Add the ancho and chipotle chilies and tomatoes and cook 5 minutes, stirring frequently. Add the water and chicken stock and bring to a boil over high heat; cook 5 minutes, stirring frequently. Reduce the heat to moderate and simmer 30 minutes, stirring occasionally. Remove from the heat and cool to room temperature.

In a blender, puree the mixture in batches until smooth. Strain through a fine wire sieve and return to the saucepan. Add the cream and bring to a boil over high heat, stirring constantly to prevent the mixture from boiling over. Reduce the heat to moderate and cook 15 to 20 minutes, stirring often, or until the mixture is the consistency of heavy cream. Season with salt and pepper. Add the shrimp, mix well, and remove from the heat. To serve cold, cool to room temperature and refrigerate in a tightly sealed container for at least 6 hours, or up to 3 days. Serve garnished with the parsley.

five-alarm gazpacho

Arrange a single layer of the tomatoes, cut sides down, in a large, nonstick sauté pan. Add half of the onion and sprinkle with 1 teaspoon of the salt. Cook over high heat until cut sides of tomatoes are slightly charred, 4 to 6 minutes. Remove the mixture from the pan and place in a large bowl. Repeat with the remaining tomatoes, red onion, and salt and add to the bowl.

Add the cucumber, red bell pepper, chili peppers, garlic, vinegars, and olive oil to the bowl and mix well. Let stand at room temperature for 30 minutes to 1 hour. Stir in the water.

Using a blender, purée half the mixture and strain through a fine wire mesh or sieve. Transfer to a storage container large enough to accommodate the entire batch of soup. Purée the remaining mixture with the croutons and add to the strained mixture. Mix well and season with additional salt (if necessary) and pepper. If serving immediately, add 1 cup crushed ice and mix until thoroughly melted. Alternatively, refrigerate until well chilled. Garnish with green bell pepper or chives before serving.

➤ This recipe produces a slightly thick, semichunky gazpacho. If you prefer a completely smooth version, strain both batches of soup after puréeing in the blender and omit the croutons. Conversely, if you prefer a soup with lots of body, purée the mixture along with the croutons, but omit straining it altogether.

HOTTEST 8

makes 6 to 8 servings

1 1/2 pounds ripe Roma tomatoes, halved lengthwise

1 medium red onion, thinly sliced

2 teaspoons kosher salt

1 large cucumber, peeled, seeded, and coarsely chopped

1 red bell pepper, coarsely chopped

3 bird's eye (Thai) chili peppers, stemmed and coarsely chopped

2 jalapeño chili peppers, stemmed and coarsely chopped

2 cloves garlic, coarsely chopped

3 tablespoons red wine vinegar

2 tablespoons sherry vinegar

1/4 cup extra-virgin olive oil

1 cup ice water

1 cup croutons or prepared unseasoned stuffing mix

Black pepper, to taste

1 green bell pepper, cut into tiny dice, or 1/2 cup minced chives, for garnish

Texas-Style Chili with Pinto Beans

1½ cups dry pinto beans, sorted

2 quarts water

Salt, to taste

4 each dried pasilla, ancho, and cascabel chilies

1 pound bacon

2 large onions, cut in small dice

6 cloves garlic, finely chopped

6 jalapeño peppers, finely chopped

2 pounds lean beef stew meat, finely chopped (not ground)

3 tablespoons chili powder

2 tablespoons each ground cumin, coriander, and cayenne

1 cup weak coffee

3 cups unsalted beef broth or stock

Salt and pepper, to taste

1 cup chopped cilantro or parsley, for garnish

As with most regional specialties, there are many versions of "authentic" Texas-style chili. Some cooks use beans while others insist that true chili consists of only meat, chilies, and seasonings. This version is deeply flavored, contains plump pinto beans, and uses a bit of coffee for a real cowboy flavor.
Makes 6 servings.   *Hottest: rated 9*

Soak the beans in water for 12 hours or up to 1 day, changing the water every 8 hours. Drain and place in a saucepan with 2 quarts fresh water. Bring to a boil over high heat. Reduce the heat to moderately high and cook for 55 minutes to 1 hour or until the beans are tender but not mushy. Drain and season with salt. Set aside until needed.

Cover the chilies in boiling water and soak for 4 to 6 hours or until they are soft and pliable. Remove the seeds and stems and, using a bit of the soaking liquid, purée in a blender until smooth. Set aside until needed.

In a large saucepan, cook the bacon until crisp. Remove with a slotted spoon and drain on paper towels. Discard all but ¼ cup of the bacon fat. Coarsely chop the bacon and add to the beans.

Cook the onion, garlic, and jalapeño peppers in the remaining bacon fat over moderate heat for 10 minutes, stirring from time to time. Add the meat and spices and cook over high heat for 5 minutes, stirring constantly. Add the coffee, beef broth, and the reserved puréed chilies, and bring to a boil. Reduce the heat to moderately low, and cook for 1 hour to 1½ hours, stirring from time to time. When the meat is tender, add the beans and bacon; mix gently. Cook for 15 minutes, season with pepper and more salt if needed, and serve with a garnish of chopped cilantro or parsley.

Pants-on-Fire Black Bean Soup

IF YOU PREFER A COMPLETELY VEGETARIAN VERSION OF THIS MOUTH-SEARING SOUP, SUBSTITUTE
VEGETABLE STOCK OR WATER FOR THE CHICKEN STOCK. CONVERSELY, FOR A MEATIER, MORE SUBSTANTIAL DISH,
ADD DICED SMOKED HAM OR COOKED AND CHOPPED BACON DURING THE LAST TWENTY MINUTES OF COOKING.
MAKES ABOUT 8 SERVINGS. ～ **HOTTEST #10**

Soak the beans in 8 cups of cold water overnight, changing the water once or twice. Drain the beans and place in a large, heavy-bottomed saucepan with the cascabel, de árbol, ancho, and pasilla chilies and 5 quarts of fresh water. Bring to a boil over high heat. Reduce the heat to moderate and simmer for 1 hour and 40 minutes, or until the beans are tender.

Meanwhile, in a very large, heavy-bottomed sauté pan, cook the onions, garlic, jalapeño peppers, spices, red pepper flakes, and herbs in the olive oil over moderate heat for 5 minutes, stirring constantly. Add the tomatoes and chipotle chilies and cook 5 minutes, stirring frequently. Add to the black beans along with the chicken stock; bring to a boil over high heat. Reduce the heat to moderate and simmer for 30 to 40 minutes, stirring from time to time.

Remove 6 cups of the soup and puree in batches in a blender until fairly smooth. Return to the pot and mix well. Add the lime juice and season with salt and pepper. Just before serving, garnish with the cilantro.

2 cups dried black beans, washed and sorted

6 cascabel chili peppers, stemmed, seeded, and finely chopped

5 de árbol or cayenne chili peppers, stemmed

3 ancho chili peppers, stemmed, seeded, and finely chopped

1 pasilla chili pepper, stemmed, seeded, and finely chopped

2 medium onions, cut into small dice

4 cloves garlic, finely chopped

4 jalapeño chili peppers, stemmed, seeded, and coarsely chopped

1 tablespoon each ground cumin and coriander

2½ teaspoons dried red pepper flakes

1½ teaspoons each dried oregano and sage

3 tablespoons olive or vegetable oil

2 tomatoes, cored and finely chopped

2 tablespoons canned chipotle chili peppers in adobo sauce, minced

6 cups chicken stock

½ cup fresh lime juice

Salt and pepper, to taste

1 cup coarsely chopped fresh cilantro

golden masa cakes with fresh and dried chili peppers

Soak the ancho and chipotle chilies in warm water to cover 1 to 1½ hours, or until soft and pliable. Finely chop and set aside.

In a large bowl, combine the *masa harina*, chili powder, salt, and baking powder. Add the water, cayenne chilies, and reserved chopped chilies. Mix well with a large fork until a dough forms. Add the cheese and mix with your hands to thoroughly combine ingredients and form a smooth, pliable dough. Shape the dough into a long cylinder, approximately 1 inch in diameter. Wrap tightly in plastic wrap and refrigerate for at least 2 hours, or up to 8 hours.

Thirty minutes prior to cooking, remove dough from refrigerator and slice into 20 equal pieces. When pliable, use your hands to pat each piece into a small cake.

In a large, nonstick sauté pan, heat about ½ inch of oil over moderate heat until hot but not smoking. Arrange a single layer of masa cakes in the oil, leaving approximately ¾ inch of space between each one. Cook until golden brown on bottoms, 3 or 4 minutes. Gently flip cakes using a spatula, and cook second sides until golden brown. Remove with slotted spatula and drain on paper towels. Cook remaining cakes in this fashion, adding more oil as needed. Serve immediately, garnished with sprigs of cilantro.

➤ For lunch or a light supper, pair these tasty little cakes with a salad of finely shredded cabbage, carrots, and red onions spiked with vinegar and dried oregano. For an hors d'oeuvre, serve with a platter of assorted Mexican cheeses, sliced jicama (a Latin American root vegetable), various salsas, guacamole and tortilla chips.

HOTTEST 7

makes 20 cakes; about 6 servings

2 ancho chili peppers, stemmed and seeded

2 chipotle chili peppers, stemmed and seeded

2 cups *masa harina* (Mexican cornmeal)

2 teaspoons dried chili powder

1½ teaspoons kosher salt

1 scant teaspoon baking powder

1 cup warm water

2 thick cayenne or Las Cruces chili peppers, stemmed, seeded, and minced

½ pound Monterey Jack cheese, finely grated

⅓ cup vegetable or peanut oil, for cooking

Sprigs of cilantro, for garnish

corn pudding with sweet and hot chilies

3 large ears corn, kernels shaved (about 2 1/2 cups corn kernels)

3 hot cherry chili peppers, stemmed, seeded, and coarsely chopped

2 Hungarian sweet chili peppers, stemmed and coarsely chopped

2 bird's eye (Thai) chili peppers, stemmed and finely chopped

3 tablespoons unsalted butter

2 teaspoons dried chili powder

1 teaspoon minced chipotle chili pepper

1 1/4 cups heavy whipping cream

3 eggs, separated

2 teaspoons kosher or sea salt

1 teaspoon black pepper

➤ How can you go wrong with a dish that contains mild and hot chili peppers, fresh sweet corn, and cream? If you're like me, you may find it difficult to keep yourself from eating the entire dish. Serve with sliced tomatoes garnished with fresh basil or a summer vegetable salad of steamed sugar snap peas, English green peas, and asparagus.

HOTTER 6
makes 4 to 6 servings

Preheat oven to 350° F. Generously grease a 2-quart ovenproof baking dish.

Place the corn in a large bowl. In a large sauté pan, heat the hot cherry, Hungarian, and bird's eye chili peppers over high heat 1½ to 2 minutes, until any liquid has evaporated and they are slightly limp. Add the butter and stir until melted. Remove from the heat and add to the corn, along with the chili powder, chipotle, whipping cream, egg yolks, salt, and pepper; mix well.

Using an electric mixer, beat the egg whites in a medium bowl until stiff but not dry. Gently fold into the corn mixture just until blended. Do not overmix. Turn mixture into prepared dish.

Set the baking dish in a large, ovenproof pan. Add hot water until it reaches halfway up the side of the pan. Place in the center of the oven and bake 45 to 50 minutes, or until a knife inserted into the center comes out clean. Remove from the oven and let stand at room temperature 5 to 7 minutes before serving.

baked polenta with chili peppers and smoked cheese

6 cups homemade vegetable stock (page 13) or canned vegetable broth (preferably low-sodium)

2 tablespoons unsalted butter

1 1/2 cups coarse cornmeal

1 large California green or poblano chili pepper, stemmed, seeded, and finely chopped

3 red jalapeño or bird's eye (Thai) chili peppers, stemmed, seeded, and finely chopped

1 teaspoon cumin seeds

1/2 pound naturally smoked Cheddar or mozzarella cheese, finely grated

Salt and pepper, to taste

Vegetable oil, for brushing

Fresh herb sprigs, for garnish

➤ Team this delectable, chili-spiked polenta with a salad of lightly dressed mixed greens tossed with marinated artichoke hearts and green beans to make a well-rounded meal.

This recipe requires chilling the polenta for at least four hours before baking to allow it to set. If you don't have the time for this, you may eliminate the molding and baking steps and serve the polenta soft, spooned into a shallow bowl.

HOTTER 4

makes 8 servings

Lightly grease eight 1-cup molds or one 9-x-13-inch baking dish (for making diamond or square shapes).

In a large, heavy-bottomed saucepan, bring the vegetable stock and butter to a boil over high heat. Add the cornmeal, whisking constantly with a wire whisk for the first 5 to 7 minutes to form a smooth mixture. Reduce the heat to moderate and continue cooking, stirring constantly with a wooden spoon, 7 to 10 minutes or until the mixture is thick and smooth. Add the chili peppers and cumin and cook 7 to 10 minutes longer, stirring frequently, until very thick and aromatic.

Add the cheese, remove from the heat, and stir well until melted. Season with salt and pepper and immediately pour into prepared molds or a baking dish. (At this point, it may also be poured into a bowl and served soft.) Brush surface of polenta with a thin coat of vegetable oil and cover tightly with plastic wrap. Refrigerate for at least 6 hours or up to 24 hours.

Preheat oven to 400° F. Turn out polenta from individual molds and place on a large baking sheet or, if you used a 9-x-13-inch dish, cut polenta into 2-inch squares, rectangles, or diamond shapes and place on baking sheet. Bake 15 to 20 minutes, or until heated through and light golden brown. Serve immediately, garnished with fresh herbs.

African BERBERE *Sauce*

Berbere, THE OFFICIAL LANGUAGE OF ETHIOPIA, IS ALSO THE NAME GIVEN TO THIS INCENDIARY RED PEPPER SAUCE. USED BOTH AS A TABLE CONDIMENT AND AS AN INGREDIENT IN MANY SOUPS, STEWS, MARINADES, AND MEAT DISHES, *BERBERE* PLAYS A VERY IMPORTANT ROLE IN THE COOKING OF ETHIOPIA, AND CAN BE A VALUABLE INGREDIENT FOR AMERICAN COOKS, AS WELL.

When you prepare this intoxicating, brick-red chili sauce, be sure to use your overhead stove fan or open all the windows. You might also want to tie a scarf around your nose and mouth while heating the spices in the sauté pan.

MAKES ABOUT 2 CUPS. ∼ **HOTTEST #9**

Place the red pepper flakes, cumin, black pepper, salt, cardamom, fenugreek, nutmeg, cloves, cinnamon, allspice, and coriander in a medium, heavy-bottomed nonstick sauté pan. Cook over moderate heat, stirring constantly, until their aroma fills the air and the color has darkened slightly, about 4 minutes. Transfer to a blender and set aside.

In the same pan, heat the cayenne pepper and paprika over moderately low heat for 4 to 5 minutes, stirring constantly. Add to the spice mixture in the blender along with the garlic, water, and peanut oil. Puree until smooth, stopping occasionally to scrape the sides of the container.

Return the pureed mixture to the sauté pan and cook over moderately low heat for 10 to 12 minutes, stirring frequently to prevent the sauce from burning. Remove from the heat and cool to room temperature. Store in a tightly sealed container in the refrigerator for up to 5 months.

3 to 5 tablespoons dried red pepper flakes

2 teaspoons each ground cumin, black pepper, and kosher or sea salt

½ teaspoon each ground cardamom, fenugreek, nutmeg, cloves, cinnamon, allspice, and coriander

1¼ cups cayenne pepper

3 tablespoons paprika

6 cloves garlic, minced

2 cups water

3 tablespoons peanut oil

flaming-hot habanero chili pepper sauce

In a large, nonstick sauté pan, cook the onion and garlic over high heat 5 minutes, stirring frequently. Add the chili peppers and cook 5 to 7 minutes, stirring frequently, until the onions are blackened around the edges and the chilies are limp. Add the water and vinegar, reduce heat to moderately high, and cook 5 minutes. Remove from heat and cool slightly.

Transfer to a food processor and process, pulsing on and off, until uniformly minced. Season with salt and pepper and add cilantro, if desired. Store in a tightly sealed nonreactive container in the refrigerator up to 1 month.

➤ Although this is one of the most fierce chili pepper sauces I have sampled, it also has a tremendous amount of flavor and depth. Remember: *a little bit goes a long way!* Spoon a little on fried or scrambled eggs, or use it to add pizzazz to rice, pasta, or grain dishes.

HOTTEST 10+

makes about 1 ½ cups

1 large onion, halved and thinly sliced

5 cloves garlic

12 habanero chili peppers, stemmed

4 thick cayenne or hot goat horn chili peppers, stemmed and coarsely chopped

2 pimento or apple chili peppers, stemmed and coarsely chopped

1 cup water

¼ cup white wine vinegar or apple cider vinegar

Salt and pepper, to taste

⅓ cup minced fresh cilantro, optional

Zhoug—*Israeli Chili Pepper Paste*

Sizzling hot and fragrant with fresh herbs, this snappy jalapeño paste
can be used with grilled meats, fish, and poultry; as a booster for soups and stews;
or mixed with fresh, finely chopped tomatoes, as they do in the Middle East.

Makes about 1 cup. *Hottest #7*

12 green jalapeño chili peppers, stemmed and seeded

3 cloves garlic

¾ cup loosely packed fresh parsley leaves

½ cup loosely packed fresh cilantro leaves

1½ tablespoons water

1½ teaspoons each ground cumin and cayenne pepper

1 teaspoon each kosher salt and pepper

Place the jalapeño peppers and garlic in the bowl of a food processor. Process until smooth. Add the parsley, cilantro, water, spices, salt, and pepper. Process until smooth. Transfer to a nonreactive container, cover tightly, and store in the refrigerator for up to 3 months.

spring vegetable stir-fry with mild and hot chilies

Bring a small pot of salted water to boil over high heat. Remove the fava beans from the shell (you should have about 1 cup). Add the beans to the water and cook 2 minutes. Drain in a colander and cool to room temperature. Using your fingers, gently snip the outer skin on the tip of each fava bean; gently squeeze the bean from the outer skin. Discard skins and set fava beans aside.

In a very large sauté pan, cook the asparagus and sugar peas in the olive oil over moderate heat for 3 minutes, stirring occasionally. Add the chili peppers, fava beans, and sherry and cook over high heat 2 to 3 minutes, or until all the vegetables are tender. Add the garlic chives and vinegar and cook 15 to 20 seconds, stirring constantly. Season with salt and pepper and serve immediately.

➤ This is a lovely dish to serve on a warm spring or summer evening. Accompany with warm rolls and butter and an oaky chardonnay or chilled sherry.

HOT 1

makes 4 to 6 servings

1 1/2 pounds fresh fava beans in the shell

1 pound asparagus, bottoms trimmed, sliced on the diagonal into 1-inch-long pieces

3/4 pound sugar snap peas, ends trimmed and stringed

1 1/2 tablespoons olive oil

3 apple or small pimento chili peppers, stemmed, seeded, and quartered

2 red jalapeño or hot cherry chili peppers, stemmed, seeded, and thinly sliced

3 tablespoons dry sherry

1 bunch garlic chives or scallions, finely chopped

Splash sherry vinegar or champagne vinegar

Salt and pepper, to taste

Burmese Beef and Potato Coconut Curry

TENDER BEEF CHUNKS AND POTATOES ACCENTED WITH AROMATIC SPICES, ASSORTED HOT CHILI PEPPERS, AND SWEET COCONUT MILK MELD TOGETHER IN THIS RICH AND SATISFYING STEW. SERVE WITH STEAMED RICE AND STIR-FRIED GREEN BEANS.
MAKES 6 SERVINGS. ⌁ HOTTEST #9

5 tablespoons peanut oil

2 pounds beef stew meat, cut into 1-inch cubes

2 medium onions, cut into large dice

4 cloves garlic, finely chopped

8 serrano chili peppers, stemmed and thinly sliced

5 jalapeño chili peppers, stemmed, seeded, and thinly sliced

1 tablespoon each ground cumin and coriander

2 teaspoons each ground fennel seeds and turmeric

1½ teaspoons cayenne pepper

Two 13½-ounce cans unsweetened coconut milk

1 cup water

3 medium boiling potatoes (about 1 pound), peeled and cut into ½-inch cubes

½ cup fresh lime juice

Salt and pepper, to taste

3 red serrano chili peppers (or any other small red chili pepper), stemmed and thinly sliced

½ cup finely chopped fresh cilantro, for garnish

In a very large nonstick sauté pan, heat 2 tablespoons of the oil over high heat. Add the beef and cook, stirring frequently, until golden brown on all sides. Remove with a slotted spoon and set aside.

In the same pan, add the remaining 3 tablespoons oil and heat until hot but not smoking. Add the onions, garlic, chili peppers, and spices and cook 7 to 8 minutes, stirring frequently. Transfer to a large, heavy-bottomed pot and add the beef. Cook the mixture over high heat for 3 minutes, stirring constantly.

Add the coconut milk and water and bring to a boil. Reduce the heat to moderate and cook 1 hour and 15 minutes, or until the meat is very tender. Add the potatoes and lime juice and cook 10 to 12 minutes, or until the potatoes are tender when pierced with a fork. Season with salt and pepper. Just before serving, garnish with the serrano chilies and cilantro.

fiery east african vegetable and lentil stew

1 large onion, cut into dice

4 cloves garlic, finely chopped

4 bird's eye (Thai) or serrano chili peppers, stemmed and thinly sliced

1 1/2 tablespoons cayenne pepper

1 tablespoon *each* ground cumin and coriander seeds

1/2 teaspoon *each* ground cinnamon and cloves

4 tablespoons *ghee* or clarified unsalted butter (see note, page 53)

2 cups peeled, seeded, and chopped tomatoes

3/4 cup washed and sorted lentils

6 cups homemade vegetable stock (page 13) or canned vegetable broth (preferably low-sodium)

2 red potatoes, cut into dice

1 large carrot, cut into 1/2-inch pieces

2 cups tightly packed, washed and trimmed collard greens, cut into 1/4-inch strips

Salt and pepper, to taste

3 hard-cooked eggs, halved, for garnish

➤ This robust stew has so much body and flavor, not to mention nutritional value, even nonvegetarians will relish its deliciously hearty qualities.

HOTTEST 8

makes about 6 servings

In a large, heavy-bottomed pot, cook the onion, garlic, chili peppers, cayenne, cumin, coriander, cinnamon, and cloves in the *ghee* over moderate heat 5 to 7 minutes, stirring frequently. Add the tomatoes, lentils, and vegetable stock and bring to a boil over high heat. Reduce the heat to moderate and simmer 40 to 45 minutes, stirring occasionally, until the lentils are tender.

Add the potatoes, carrots, and collard greens and cook 12 to 15 minutes, or until all the vegetables are tender. Season with salt and pepper. Serve hot, garnished with the hard-cooked eggs.

potato-cheese tacos with three chilies

Preheat oven to 400° F.

Bake potatoes in center of oven 45 to 50 minutes, or until tender when pierced with a fork. Remove from oven and cool to room temperature. Slice in half and scrape the pulp into a large bowl; gently crumble with a fork. (Do not mash the potatoes or they will be gummy.)

To the potatoes add the cheese, chili peppers, egg, and cilantro; mix gently with a fork until thoroughly combined. Cover tightly with plastic wrap and refrigerate for 2 hours or up to 1 day.

To prepare tacos: Lay tortillas on a flat work surface. Using about 2 rounded tablespoons per tortilla, spoon the mixture onto one half of each tortilla. Fold over the second half and press gently to secure.

In a very large, nonstick sauté pan, heat about ¼ inch of oil over moderate heat until hot. Add as many tacos as will comfortably fit in the pan without crowding. Cook each side about 2 minutes, or until light golden brown and the filling is heated through. Remove with a slotted spatula and drain on paper towels. Cook the remaining tacos in this fashion, adding more oil as needed. Serve immediately, garnished with sprigs of cilantro.

➤ I find these vegetarian tacos irresistible and fun to eat.

Although they appeal to youngsters with adventurous palates, grown-ups will appreciate the homey ingredients and unique taste.

HOTTER 6
makes 4 to 6 servings

3 large baking potatoes (about 2¾ pounds)

⅓ pound sharp Cheddar cheese, finely grated

1 California green chili pepper, stemmed and finely chopped

3 red jalapeño chili peppers, stemmed, seeded, and finely chopped

1 hot goat horn or Hungarian sweet chili pepper, stemmed, seeded, and finely chopped

1 egg, lightly beaten

3 tablespoons minced fresh cilantro

10 to 12 6-inch corn tortillas

½ to ⅔ cup vegetable oil, for frying

Sprigs of cilantro, for garnish

DORO WAT—*Ethiopian Chicken Stew*

RECIPES CONTAINING THE WORD *WAT* ARE CONSIDERED NATIONAL DISHES OF ETHIOPIA. *INJERA*, THE SPONGY, BLAND, PLIABLE FLAT BREAD TRADITIONALLY SERVED WITH THIS FIERY EAST AFRICAN STEW CAN BE PURCHASED READY-MADE AT A LOCAL AFRICAN RESTAURANT, OR PREPARED FROM SCRATCH. ALTERNATELY, SERVE ITALIAN BREAD WITH THIS FLAMING HOT STEW, AND RICE OR CRACKED WHEAT AS A COMPANION.

MAKES ABOUT 4 SERVINGS. ⌒ **HOTTEST #10**

4 tablespoons unsalted butter

2 large onions, halved and cut into
½-inch-wide slices

6 cloves garlic, finely chopped

2 teaspoons cayenne pepper

1 teaspoon each ground cardamom, cumin,
fennel seeds, and nutmeg

½ cup African Berbere *Sauce (see page 29)*

¼ cup tomato paste

4 chicken thighs

4 chicken legs

2½ cups chicken stock

4 hard-cooked eggs, pierced all over ¼-inch deep
with a fork and halved

Salt and pepper, to taste

½ cup finely chopped fresh cilantro

In a very large, heavy-bottomed saucepan, melt the butter over moderate heat. Add the onions, garlic, cayenne pepper, and spices and cook 15 minutes, stirring frequently. Add the *Berbere* sauce, tomato paste, and chicken and cook 10 minutes, stirring frequently. Add the stock and bring to a boil over high heat. Reduce the heat to moderate and simmer 1 hour, or until the chicken is very tender. Add the eggs and cook 10 minutes. Season with salt and pepper. Just before serving, garnish with the cilantro.

NOTE: To make hard-cooked eggs, place room-temperature eggs in a saucepan and generously cover with cold water. Bring to a boil over high heat and cook 1½ minutes. Remove from the heat and cover tightly. Let stand at room temperature for 1 hour. Remove the eggs, rap gently on a hard surface, and peel.

African Fire Pork Stew

12 small dried red chilies

3 pounds pork butt, trimmed of excess fat and tendon, cut in 1-inch pieces (about 3 cups chopped pork meat)

2 large onions, cut in large dice

6 cloves garlic, coarsely chopped

6 jalapeño peppers, seeded, stemmed, and coarsely chopped

⅓ cup peanut oil

2-inch piece ginger root, peeled and coarsely chopped

1 tablespoon paprika

2 teaspoons each ground nutmeg, coriander, cinnamon, and allspice

2 tablespoons dark brown sugar

5 cups unsalted beef broth or stock

3 cups peeled and chopped tomatoes, or a 28-ounce can tomatoes

¾ cup roasted peanuts

4 medium sweet potatoes, peeled and cut into ¾-inch pieces

¼ cup red wine vinegar

If you are a true chili pepper enthusiast you will have to try this incendiary North African pork stew. In Africa, hot dishes are made even hotter with a sauce called berbere—a mixture of chilies, spices, and tomatoes. If you need extra heat in this stew, add a tablespoon of dried red pepper flakes or a dash of prepared hot sauce, but I would sample a few spoonfuls before adding any more chilies.
Makes 6 servings.   *Hottest: rated 9*

Cover the dried chilies in boiling water and soak for 2 to 3 hours or until they are soft. Drain and coarsely chop. Set aside until needed.

Cook the pork, onions, garlic, and jalapeño peppers in the peanut oil over high heat for 7 to 10 minutes, stirring all the while. Add the ginger, spices, and sugar and cook over moderate heat for 5 minutes, stirring frequently. Add the beef broth and bring to a boil over high heat. Add the tomatoes, peanuts, and reserved chilies, reduce the heat to moderate, and cook for 1 hour, stirring from time to time.

Add the potatoes and vinegar and cook for 25 to 30 minutes or until the meat and potatoes are tender. Season with salt and pepper and garnish with chopped parsley to taste.

Chicken Mole

Don't be scared away by the long list of ingredients—all but three are cooked together in one pot and then puréed. A good mole has layers of flavor and different intensities of heat, which come from many different chilies and long, slow cooking. It improves with age and is best the second or third day. Serve this poultry dish with rice and corn tortillas and sautéed zucchini or pattypan squash. Makes 10 to 12 servings.   *Hottest: rated 10*

To make the mole: Place the chilies, tomatoes, onion, garlic, jalapeños, spices and herbs, and water in a heavy-bottomed, large saucepan. Bring to a boil over high heat. Cook for 10 minutes, stirring frequently. Reduce the heat to moderate, and simmer for 1 to 1½ hours, or until the mixture is slightly thick and aromatic. Cool to room temperature. Purée in a blender until smooth. Strain through a wire mesh and return to the saucepan.

Add the chocolate and peanut butter and bring the sauce to a boil. Reduce the heat to low and simmer for 30 minutes, stirring frequently. Season with salt and pepper. At this point the sauce can be stored, covered, in the refrigerator for up to 1 week.

Preheat oven to 400° F.

In a large nonstick skillet, brown the chicken on all sides in batches. Divide the chicken and mole between two large baking dishes, and cover with tin foil. Bake for 45 to 50 minutes, or until the chicken is tender and cooked all the way through. Drizzle with lime juice, garnish with chopped cilantro, and serve immediately.

Note: Alternately, use only 1 large chicken plus 2 extra legs. In this case, use only half of the sauce in one baking dish, and half of the lime juice and cilantro when serving. Freeze the remaining sauce in a tightly sealed container for up to 4 months, or refrigerate for 5 days.

Mole:

4 dried pasilla chilies

4 dried ancho chilies

3 dried small Asian or Italian red chilies

3 chipotle peppers

2 dried California or nuevo Mexicana chilies

4 jalapeño peppers, stemmed, seeded, and chopped

3 medium tomatoes, chopped

1 large onion, coarsely chopped

4 cloves garlic, chopped

1 tablespoon each ground cinnamon, cumin, coriander, and black pepper

2 teaspoons each ground mace, cloves, and oregano

3½ quarts water

3 ounces semisweet chocolate

⅓ cup smooth peanut butter

Salt and pepper, to taste

2 large chickens (4 to 4½ pounds each), plus four extra legs, cut into serving pieces (see Note)

Juice from 3 limes

1½ cups chopped cilantro, for garnish

Walnut-Fig Tart with Ancho Chilies

Dough:

2 cups all-purpose flour

½ cup sugar

1 teaspoon salt

½ pound (2 sticks) chilled unsalted butter, cut into 24 chunks

3 to 5 tablespoons cold water

Filling:

5 dried pasilla or ancho chilies

2½ cups dried figs, stemmed and coarsely chopped

2 cups white wine

¾ cup sugar

4 tablespoons (½ stick) unsalted butter

¼ cup bourbon or whiskey

1 tablespoon vanilla extract

1 cup coarsely chopped walnuts

Dash cayenne pepper

Créme fraîche or vanilla ice cream (optional)

Blond dried calmyrna figs combined with dried ancho chilies makes an unusual filling for this handsome tart. The chilies blend with the sweet figs and walnuts, producing a finely balanced and unusual pastry. Serve with sherry for a unique dessert.

Makes 6 to 8 servings.   *Hot: rated 1*

To make the dough: Place the flour, sugar, and salt in a bowl; mix well. Add the butter and, with your fingers, combine just until the mixture resembles coarse meal. Add the water and form into a ball. Wrap in plastic and refrigerate for 2 hours or up to 2 days.

Cover the chilies with boiling water to cover, and let soak for 2 to 3 hours or until they are soft and pliable. Remove the seeds and stems, finely chop, and set aside until needed.

Preheat oven to 375° F.

Remove the dough from the refrigerator ½ hour before you plan to bake it. Press the dough into a 10-inch tart pan; make an even bottom layer, press up the sides, and extend a ¼- to ½-inch ridge above the top edge of the tart pan. Cover with parchment paper or foil, fill with pie weights or dried beans, and bake for 20 minutes. Remove the paper and weights, re-cover only the edges, and bake for 10 to 15 minutes more or until the crust is just turning very light brown. Remove from the oven and let cool to room temperature before filling.

Meanwhile, to prepare the filling: Place the figs, wine, and sugar in a heavy-bottomed saucepan. Bring to a boil over high heat. Reduce the heat to moderate and cook for 10 to 15 minutes or until the figs are tender and the liquid is syrupy. Add the butter, bourbon, vanilla extract, walnuts, cayenne pepper, and reserved chilies; mix well until the butter is melted. Remove from the heat and cool.

Fill the tart shell and serve, optionally with a drizzle of crèm fraîche or vanilla ice cream.

Jalapeño-Lime Ice

3 cups water

2 cups sugar

8 jalapeño peppers, coarsely chopped

1¼ cups coarsely chopped mint leaves

½ cup fresh lime juice

4 cups ice cubes

Mint sprigs, for garnish

Lime slices, for garnish

Refreshing and stimulating, this sweet-hot concoction can be served for dessert, after a spicy meal, or between courses for an unusual palate cleanser and to restore the appetite. For a more pronounced mint flavor, mince 3 tablespoons of fresh mint leaves and stir them in just before serving.
Makes 6 servings.   *Hotter: rated 6*

Place the water, sugar, jalapeño peppers, mint, and lime juice in a large, heavy-bottomed saucepan. Bring to a boil over high heat. Boil for 25 to 30 minutes, stirring frequently. Remove from the heat and cool slightly. Strain the liquid, and place in a covered nonreactive container in the freezer for 6 hours or up to 2 days. (The mixture won't freeze but will become slushy and icy.)

Using a cleaver or heavy object, slightly crush the ice cubes. Place ice cubes in a blender along with the jalapeño-lime mixture. Blend until the ice is finely crushed. Serve immediately, garnished with sprigs of fresh mint and lime slices.

frozen chocolate silk with ancho chilies

7-ounce jar marshmallow cream

³/₄ cup corn syrup

2 teaspoons vanilla extract

¹/₃ cup cold water

1 envelope unflavored gelatin

2 cups half-and-half

8 ounces unsweetened chocolate, coarsely chopped

1 cup cocoa powder

4 toasted ancho chili peppers, stemmed, seeded, and ground, or 3 tablespoons hot chili powder

¹/₂ cup toasted peanuts, finely chopped (optional)

Fresh mint sprigs, for garnish

➤ This decadent frozen confection is sure to stimulate dinner conversation—if not your taste buds. The marriage of intense chocolate and dark, dusky ancho chili peppers makes an unforgettable combination. The garnish of toasted peanuts completes the Latin American character of this enchanting dessert.

HOTTER 4

makes about 6 servings

In a large bowl, using an electric mixer, beat the marshmallow cream, corn syrup, and vanilla until smooth. Set aside.

Place the water in a small bowl. Sprinkle the gelatin over the surface and let stand at room temperature 5 minutes. Stir well until dissolved. Set aside.

Place the half-and-half, unsweetened chocolate, cocoa powder, and ancho chili powder in a heavy-bottomed saucepan. Heat over moderate heat, stirring frequently, until chocolate has melted and mixture is thoroughly combined and smooth. Remove from heat, add the gelatin mixture, and mix well.

Add one third of the chocolate mixture to the marshmallow mixture; beat well until smooth. Add the remaining chocolate mixture and beat until thoroughly combined and smooth. Transfer to a storage container with a tight-fitting lid and place in freezer until set, about 6 hours. Remove 10 minutes before serving to soften slightly. Spoon into serving bowls and garnish with peanuts, if desired, and fresh mint. Serve immediately.

Chocolate-Coffee Brownies with Chipotle Chilies

CHOCOLATE LOVERS WILL EXPERIENCE A REAL SURPRISE WHEN THEY BITE INTO THESE DENSE, RICH BROWNIES.
HOTHEADS WILL DELIGHT!

MAKES ABOUT 6 SERVINGS. ᗡ HOTTER #6

Soak the chilies in hot water for 30 minutes, or until they are soft. Drain well and set aside.

Preheat oven to 350°F. Grease and lightly flour an 8-by-8-inch baking pan.

In a small saucepan, melt the butter and 5 ounces of the chocolate over low heat, stirring frequently. Add the ground coffee and reserved chilies and mix well. Cool to room temperature.

Place the sugar and eggs in a large bowl. Using a large kitchen spoon, beat until light in color and smooth, about 2 minutes. Add the chocolate mixture. Add the flour, salt, walnuts, and remaining 3 ounces of chocolate; mix until just combined. Pour the batter into the prepared pan and smooth the surface with a dull knife.

Bake on the lower shelf of the oven for 20 minutes. Rotate to the upper shelf and bake 30 minutes, or until the center is just set. Remove from the oven and cool to room temperature. When cool, run a dull knife around the edge of the pan and cut the brownies into squares. Serve immediately or wrap tightly in plastic wrap or aluminum foil and store at room temperature for up to 3 days.

3 to 4 dried chipotle chili peppers, stemmed, seeded, and finely chopped

3 dried pepperoncini or any other tiny dried chili peppers, stemmed, seeded, and finely chopped

6 ounces unsalted butter (1½ sticks)

8 ounces semisweet chocolate, coarsely chopped

1½ tablespoons finely ground dark-roast coffee beans

1½ cups sugar

3 eggs, lightly beaten

1 cup all-purpose flour

Pinch salt

¾ cup coarsely chopped walnuts

frijoles a los angeles con salsa a diablo ◆ angelic beans with sauce of the devil

1 pound large lima beans, washed and sorted

2 ancho chili peppers, stemmed, seeded, and coarsely chopped

1 chipotle chili pepper, stemmed, seeded, and coarsely chopped

1 bay leaf

2 medium onions, coarsely chopped

16 habanero chili peppers, stemmed and coarsely chopped

3 red jalapeño or bird's eye (Thai) chili peppers, stemmed and coarsely chopped

6 cloves garlic, coarsely chopped

1 tablespoon *each* ground cumin and coriander

3 tablespoons olive oil

Salt and pepper, to taste

¹/₂ cup coarsely chopped fresh cilantro, for garnish

➤ The contrast between plump, mild-flavored white lima beans and their inferno-like sauce inspired the name for this blazing-hot bean dish. You may temper the heat by adding only half of the habanero chili peppers—which still guarantees a mouth-searing experience.

I like this dish with hot rolls spread with butter and drizzled with a little honey. You may also serve with warm corn tortillas or, for a more ample meal, cheese quesadillas made with flour tortillas.

HOTTEST 10+

makes about 8 servings

Soak the beans in 2 quarts water 8 to 12 hours, changing the water a couple of times during soaking. Drain beans in colander and place in heavy-bottomed, 8-quart saucepan. Add the ancho and chipotle chili peppers, bay leaf, and 5½ quarts of cold water. Bring to a boil over high heat, stirring frequently. Reduce heat to moderate and simmer 1½ hours, stirring occasionally.

In a very large sauté pan, cook the onions, habanero and jalapeño chili peppers, garlic, cumin, and coriander in the olive oil over high heat 5 to 7 minutes, stirring frequently. Using a large ladle, remove 2 cups of the bean cooking liquid and add to the onion-chili mixture. Cook 3 minutes, stirring constantly, until slightly thick. Remove from the heat, add 2 more cups of bean cooking liquid and cool slightly. Using a blender, purée the chili mixture in batches until nearly smooth. Add to the beans and mix well.

Cook the beans 45 to 50 minutes longer, stirring occasionally, until very tender. (If beans require still more cooking, add a little more water.) Season with salt and pepper. Serve garnished with cilantro.

Chocolate-Chili Cake with Mocha Frosting

3 large dried ancho chilies

3 chipotle peppers

½ cup water

½ pound (2 sticks) unsalted butter

4 ounces unsweetened chocolate

½ cup Dutch process cocoa

2 large eggs, at room temperature

2½ cups granulated sugar

1 cup buttermilk

1 tablespoon almond extract

2 cups all-purpose flour

1 teaspoon baking soda

1 tablespoon ground cinnamon

¼ teaspoon salt

Mocha Frosting:

8 ounces bittersweet chocolate

2 tablespoons water

½ pound (2 sticks) unsalted butter, softened

1 tablespoon very finely ground dark roast coffee

3 cups confectioner's sugar

1½ cups coarsely chopped toasted almonds, for garnish

This dessert combination of bittersweet chocolate and dusky dried chilies isn't so strange when you consider their happy pairing in Mexican mole sauce. This is a sort of reverse mole sauce—heavy on the sweet and chocolate, light on the spicy essence of chili peppers. If you have the same passions for chocolate and hot chilies that I do, you won't be disappointed by this exotic cake recipe.
Makes 8 to 10 servings. Hot: rated 2

Preheat oven to 350° F.

Soak the chilies in water to cover overnight or until soft and pliable. Remove the seeds and stems and discard the water. Using a blender, purée the ancho chilies and the chipotle peppers in the ½ cup water until smooth.

Melt the butter and chocolate with the cocoa over low heat, stirring often until butter and chocolate are completely melted. Place the eggs, sugar, buttermilk, and almond extract in a large bowl; mix well. Add the dry ingredients (no need to sift) to the buttermilk mixture and mix well. Add the butter-chocolate mixture and the chilies; mix well.

Grease and flour 3 cake pans. Distribute the batter evenly among the pans. Bake for 25 to 30 minutes or until a toothpick inserted in the center comes out clean. Let cakes cool before removing from the pans.

To make the Mocha Frosting: Melt the chocolate and the water over very low heat until the chocolate is melted, stir to combine, and cool to room temperature. Combine the chocolate, butter, and coffee in a bowl. Add the sugar and beat at high speed with an electric mixer until the mixture is smooth and creamy.

Assemble the cake by placing one layer on a large plate. Frost the top, cover with second layer, frost the top of it, and top with last layer. Frost the top of the cake and the sides. Garnish the edges with the almonds.

ginger

$\mathcal{G}$INGER

Until fairly recently, many Americans considered fresh ginger an exotic ingredient. Now, however, cooks are borrowing from the many cultures that have traditionally used the flavorful root in their cookery. Highly treasured by Asian and Indian cooks, both fresh and powdered ginger also frequently appear in the cuisines of Africa and the Caribbean. Although in this country ginger has generally been reserved for preparing these ethnic cuisines, inventive American chefs have broadened the use of fresh ginger root by incorporating it into other cuisines and by pairing it with new and unexpected ingredients.

Ginger plants grow best when planted in rich sandy soil in hot, humid, rainy climates. Hawaii, Fiji, the Caribbean, Costa Rica, Guatemala, Nicaragua, Australia, India, and China are the primary growers of fresh ginger. China and India are the biggest producers and exporters of powdered ginger, a form used primarily for baked goods and in beverages. Crystallized ginger is usually eaten as a candy or as an after-dinner palate refresher, but it is also used for decorating and garnishing baked goods and other confections. Vinegared ginger is a mainstay of Japanese cuisine that is most often paired with sushi or sashimi.

Fresh ginger root is versatile and easy to use in both sweet and savory dishes. Depending on how it is used, the flavor of ginger can range from bitingly sharp and spicy to mild and gently warm. As a result, it is compatible with a wide assortment of foods. Reflecting the multifaceted quality of this rhizome, the recipes in this chapter are not limited to Asian or Indian fare, nor are all recipes exceedingly fiery.

Warmed, rather than set afire by fresh ginger, are such dishes as *Gingered Spring Vegetable and Salmon Soup, Cold Noodles and Asian Vegetables with Ginger Peanut Sauce*, and the moist and delicious *Spiced Ginger Cake with Candied Ginger Cream*. Hotter and more piquant are such traditional dishes as *Chinese Stir-Fried Beef with Ginger* and *Apricot-Ginger Chutney*. The icy-hot *Apple, Ginger, and Mint Sorbet* also packs quite a punch!

When purchasing fresh ginger, look for very hard roots with smooth, unblemished, light brown skin; the "hand," as the root is often referred to, should not yield to finger pressure and ought to be free of cuts or dents. Like other fresh produce, it's best to use ginger as soon as possible, but if you need to store it, wrap it tightly in plastic wrap and store in the vegetable bin of your refrigerator. When stored in this manner, fresh ginger will retain its flavor and texture for up to two weeks. It can be stored longer with some success, but rhizomes way past their prime are dry and flavorless.

When eating or cooking with fresh ginger, always remove the outer skin; exceptions to this principle include recipes in which ginger is used for flavoring only and removed at the end of cooking. Young ginger, which is less common in markets, does not require peeling since the skin is very thin and mild tasting and therefore edible.

To PEEL GINGER: Using a sharp paring knife, carefully remove the tough, outer layer of light brown skin and discard. If you are using the entire "hand," first remove the nubs or branches to facilitate peeling.

To CUT GINGER INTO SLIVERS: Peel the root and cut at an angle to produce oval shapes about ⅛ inch thick. Lay the flat oval shapes on the cutting board so that they barely overlap. Cutting the long way on the oval, slice into very thin, long pieces.

To FINELY CHOP GINGER: Peel the root, cut lengthwise into thin strips, and continue chopping until the ginger pieces are uniformly smaller than ⅛ inch.

To MINCE GINGER: Peel the root, cut lengthwise into thin strips, and continue chopping until the ginger is cut into minuscule pieces.

To DICE GINGER: Peel the root and slice one very thin piece from one side. Lay the root on the cutting board on the flat, cut side. Slice the root lengthwise; ⅛ inch wide for very small dice, ¼ inch wide for medium dice, and ½ inch wide for large dice. Stack the slices of ginger and cut again lengthwise into the desired-size strips. Make the final cuts by slicing across into the appropriate-size dice.

To GRATE GINGER: Peel the root and grate on a metal grater. Use the finest setting if you want mostly juice, medium for some pulp and a little juice, and the jumbo or coarsest setting for small bits of the root.

The circumference of ginger roots can be as thick as a silver dollar and as narrow as a nickel, but most roots are about the thickness of a quarter. The recipes following specify amounts in length measurements, and since this isn't exact, following are yields in standard cup measures for varying lengths of an average-size ginger root when finely chopped. You really don't have to use exact measurements of ginger, but some cooks feel better with more specific guidelines.

2-INCH PIECE GINGER ROOT = ABOUT 3 TABLESPOONS, FINELY CHOPPED

4-INCH PIECE GINGER ROOT = ABOUT ½ CUP, FINELY CHOPPED

6-INCH PIECE GINGER ROOT = ABOUT ⅔ CUP, FINELY CHOPPED

8-INCH PIECE GINGER ROOT = ABOUT 1 CUP, FINELY CHOPPED

caramelized shallot, fig, and ginger conserve

In a large, nonstick shallow-sided saucepan, cook the shallots in the butter and peanut oil over moderately low heat 20 to 25 minutes, stirring occasionally, until golden brown and very soft. Add the figs, ginger, sherry, and water and bring to a boil over high heat, stirring frequently. Reduce the heat to moderately low and cook 20 minutes, stirring occasionally, until figs are tender and mixture is thick and aromatic.

Remove from heat and cool to room temperature before serving or storing. Will keep in a tightly sealed container in the refrigerator for up to 3 weeks.

➤ Spread this sweet-spicy condiment on bread or crackers and serve with slivers of Cheddar or blue cheese. You may also add it to cooked rice, pasta, or grains to add zest, body, and flavor.

HOT 3

makes about 1 ½ cups

8 large shallots, peeled and quartered

1 ½ tablespoons unsalted butter

1 tablespoon peanut or vegetable oil

8 ounces dried Calimyrna figs, stemmed and quartered

4-inch piece fresh ginger root, peeled, quartered, and thinly sliced crosswise

½ cup dry sherry

½ cup water

spiced ginger, pear, and tomato relish

In a large sauté pan, cook the pears, tomatoes, ginger, and spices over high heat 3 minutes, stirring constantly. Add 1 cup of the water and 2 tablespoons of the honey and cook 15 minutes, stirring frequently, until liquid has almost evaporated. Add remaining cup water, remaining 2 tablespoons honey, and the salt. Cook 10 minutes, stirring frequently, until the liquid has evaporated and mixture is thick and soft. Remove from heat and cool to room temperature before storing. Store in a tightly sealed container in the refrigerator for up to 3 weeks.

➤ At once sweet, savory, and prickly with heat, this lively condiment is terrific served with grilled vegetables, baked winter squash, or braised eggplant. This relish makes an ordinary sandwich extraordinary when spread on whole-wheat bread, topped with Gruyère cheese and placed under the broiler until melted and bubbly.

HOTTER 4

makes about 1 ¼ cups

3 firm but ripe pears, stemmed, cored, and finely chopped

6 Roma tomatoes, cored and finely chopped

4-inch piece fresh ginger root, peeled and finely chopped

1 scant teaspoon *each* ground allspice, cloves, anise seeds, mace, and black pepper

2 cups water

¼ cup honey

Pinch salt

Ginger Squash Soup

2 pounds winter squash (Hubbard, acorn, butternut, or pumpkin)

1 onion, cut in medium dice

2 cloves garlic, minced

1 tablespoon ground coriander seed

1 teaspoon ground allspice

3 tablespoons olive oil

4 tablespoons (½ stick) unsalted butter

6-inch piece ginger root, peeled and coarsely chopped

1½ quarts light chicken stock

Salt and pepper, to taste

¾ cup crème fraîche (or sour cream thinned with water), for garnish

Pansies or other edible flowers, for garnish (optional)

Aromatic and pleasantly sweet, this gold-colored winter squash soup makes a heartwarming fall or winter lunch. Serve with country-style bread and a green salad.
Makes 6 servings.   Hot: rated 2

Preheat oven to 425°F.

Cut the squash in half lengthwise, seed it, and place cut side down in a shallow baking dish. Add water to a depth of 2 inches. Bake for 25 to 30 minutes or until the squash is tender. Remove from the oven and cool to room temperature. When cool enough to handle, remove the pulp from the skin and place in a bowl. Set aside until needed.

In a very large pot, cook the onion, garlic, and spices in the olive oil and butter over moderate heat for 15 minutes, stirring frequently. Add the ginger, reserved squash, and chicken stock and bring to a boil over high heat. Cook for 5 minutes, stirring constantly. Remove from the heat and cool to room temperature.

Purée the soup in batches, using a blender. Strain through a fine wire mesh and return to the saucepan. Bring to a boil over high heat; cook for 10 minutes, and season with salt and pepper. Drizzle crème fraîche, float pansies (if using them), and serve hot.

Gingered Spring Vegetable and Salmon Soup

ACCENTED WITH FRESH GINGER, THE BRILLIANT COLORS AND WELCOMING FLAVOR OF
SPRING VEGETABLES FORM THE PERFECT BACKDROP FOR TENDER NEW POTATOES AND SUCCULENT
CHUNKS OF FRESH SALMON IN THIS MEMORABLE SOUP.

MAKES ABOUT 6 SERVINGS. ~ **HOT #1**

1 teaspoon saffron threads

½ cup dry white wine

6 cups clam juice

2 shallots, halved and thinly sliced

6-inch piece fresh ginger root, peeled and slivered

6 tiny red new potatoes, quartered

*1 pound boneless salmon filet, cut into
1-inch cubes*

*1 small red bell pepper, stemmed, seeded, and
cut into tiny triangles or squares*

*6 spears asparagus, trimmed and sliced on the
diagonal into ½-inch-long pieces*

*1 large ear white corn, shaved (about 1 cup
corn kernels)*

*4 tablespoons unsalted butter, cut into 8 pieces
(optional)*

Salt and pepper, to taste

In a small bowl, dissolve the saffron in the wine by rubbing the threads together until the liquid is orange and aromatic.

In a 4-quart saucepan, place the saffron-wine mixture, clam juice, shallots, and ginger. Bring to a boil over high heat and cook 5 minutes, stirring occasionally. Add the potatoes, reduce the heat to moderately high, and cook 15 or 20 minutes, or until they are tender when pierced with a fork. Add the salmon and cook 2 minutes. Add the red bell pepper, asparagus, corn, and butter (if desired) and cook 1½ minutes, or until the salmon is just cooked. Take care not to overcook the salmon. Season with salt and pepper and serve immediately.

Spicy Ginger Syrup

2 pounds ginger root, sliced into ½-inch pieces

1 stick cinnamon

7 quarts cold water

6 cups sugar

When I was traveling in Southeast Asia, I spent many an afternoon sipping icy ginger drinks made from what tasted like pure ginger and carbonated water. Upon returning home, I decided to make my own ginger syrup. With this sweet but hot syrup you can make your own ginger ale and brighten desserts, or use it to flavor vodka and sweeten tea and in sauces, marinades, and meat or poultry glazes.
Makes about 3 cups.   *Hot: rated 2*

Place the ginger, cinnamon, and 4 quarts of the water in an 8- or 10-quart heavy-bottomed pan. Bring to a boil over high heat. Boil for 45 minutes, stirring occasionally. Add the remaining water and boil for 45 minutes. Cool slightly, strain, and return the liquid to the pan.

Add the sugar to the liquid, bring to a boil, and cook over high heat for 20 to 30 minutes, or until the liquid is thick and syrupy. (Do not leave the pot unattended, as the syrup tends to boil over.) Remove from the heat and cool to room temperature before storing in a tightly sealed glass container. Store in the refrigerator for up to 3 months.

To use Spicy Ginger Syrup: Add 2 tablespoons to a glass of tonic or sparkling water, and ice, and mix well. For desserts: Drizzle syrup over poached or fresh fruit or over sliced cake, or use it as a glaze for tarts.

Gingered Chicken Liver Spread with Currants

BRIGHT-TASTING FRESH GINGER PROVIDES AN EXCELLENT COUNTERBALANCE TO THE RICH FLAVOR AND DENSE TEXTURE OF CHICKEN LIVERS. SERVE THIS SPREAD WITH CRACKERS, CROUTONS, OR TOASTED BREAD AND A SMALL BOWL OF CORNICHONS.

MAKES 6 TO 8 SERVINGS. ❧ HOT #1

In a small bowl, soak the currants in the sherry for 30 minutes at room temperature. Drain the currants, reserving the sherry. Set both aside until needed.

In a large sauté pan, cook the onion and garlic in the olive oil over moderate heat for 5 minutes, stirring frequently. Add the reserved sherry and cook until the liquid has evaporated, 3 to 4 minutes. Add the chicken livers and coriander and cook 5 to 6 minutes, or until the livers are tender and barely pink in the center. Add the ginger and soy sauce and mix well. Remove from the heat and cool slightly.

Place the mixture in a food processor. Pulsing on and off, process the mixture until smooth. If you do not have a food processor, place the mixture on a flat cutting board, and, using a large knife or cleaver, finely mince until the mixture is smooth.

Transfer to a bowl and add the reserved currants; mix well. Season with salt and pepper. Place a piece of plastic wrap directly on the surface of the spread, cover tightly, and refrigerate for at least 4 hours or up to 4 days.

½ cup currants

¾ cup dry sherry

1 medium onion, coarsely chopped

2 cloves garlic, coarsely chopped

3 tablespoons olive oil

1 pound chicken livers, coarsely chopped

2 teaspoons ground coriander

3-inch piece fresh ginger root, peeled and minced

1 tablespoon soy sauce

Salt and pepper, to taste

gingered tomato essence with tofu silk

Soak the mushrooms in warm water 30 to 40 minutes, or until soft and pliable. Drain well. Rinse under cold running water, removing any grit or sand. Slice into very thin strips and set aside.

In a 4-quart, heavy-bottomed pan, place the tomatoes, ginger, and salt. Cook over high heat, crushing the tomatoes and stirring frequently, 12 or 13 minutes, or until the liquid has evaporated and the mixture is slightly thick. Add the water and sake and bring to a boil. Reduce the heat to moderate and simmer 50 to 55 minutes, stirring occasionally. Strain through a fine wire mesh or sieve one or two times or until no seeds remain.

Return the mixture to the pan, and bring to a boil over high heat. Add the reserved mushrooms and the scallions and cook 5 minutes. Add the tofu and cook 3 minutes. Season with salt and pepper and ladle into serving bowls. Serve immediately.

➤ Your palate may be fooled by the richly robust flavor and voluptuous texture of this surprisingly low-fat Japanese-style soup.

In peak season use fresh tomatoes from your garden or local produce stand; off-season use fresh cherry tomatoes instead.

HOTTER 6

makes 6 to 8 servings

6 dried shiitake mushrooms, stemmed

3 pounds large cherry tomatoes, stemmed

5-inch piece fresh ginger root, peeled and finely chopped

1 teaspoon kosher salt

6 cups water

2 cups sake or dry vermouth

3 scallions, green part only, finely chopped

14 ounces soft tofu (1 block), cut into 1/4-inch cubes

Salt and pepper, to taste

gingered beet and fennel salad

3 large beets, trimmed and halved

1/2 cup fresh orange juice

1 1/2 tablespoons sherry vinegar or red wine vinegar

3 tablespoons almond or peanut oil

4-inch piece fresh ginger root, peeled and slivered

1 teaspoon ground coriander

Watercress, for lining plate

2 bulbs fennel, trimmed, cored, and thinly sliced

1/3 cup toasted almonds, coarsely chopped, for garnish

➤ You may do some of the preparation for this eye-catching salad a day or two ahead, by marinating the cooked beets in the prepared dressing. Add the fennel and almonds at the last minute, then arrange atop the watercress.

HOT 3

makes about 6 servings

Place beets in a large saucepan and cover with cold water. Bring to a boil over high heat. Reduce the heat to moderately high, cover, and cook 45 to 50 minutes, or until tender when pierced with a fork. Drain well and cool to room temperature. When cool enough to handle, peel and slice into 1/4-inch wedges.

To make dressing, in a small bowl combine the orange juice, vinegar, oil, ginger, and coriander; mix well.

Place watercress on a large plate or platter. Arrange beets and fennel atop the watercress, and drizzle with the dressing.

Garnish with the almonds and serve immediately.

apple-carrot slaw with ginger-mint dressing

3 tablespoons seasoned rice
wine vinegar

2 tablespoons peanut oil

2 large Asian pears, cored
and slivered

2 medium carrots, peeled
and slivered

3-inch piece fresh ginger
root, peeled and slivered

2 shallots, thinly sliced

Salt and pepper, to taste

1/3 cup finely chopped fresh
mint

1/2 cup toasted peanuts,
coarsely chopped, for garnish

➤ Invigorating, refresh-
ing, and lusty in flavor, this
Southeast Asian–style salad is
very low in calories and fat yet
very satisfying. It can be made
completely fat-free by omitting
the peanut oil and peanuts.

Asian pears, sometimes called
apple–pears, can be found
year-round in most upscale
produce markets, full-service
grocery stores, natural food
stores, and Asian markets. If
you can't find Asian pears, use
slightly underripe European
pears such as Bartlett or Anjou;
very firm Bosc pears are also
an excellent substitute.

HOT 3
makes 4 to 6 servings

In a large bowl, whisk together the vinegar and peanut oil to form a smooth emulsion. Add the pears, carrots, ginger, and shallots; mix gently. Season with salt and pepper. (The salad can be prepared to this point and refrigerated for up to 3 hours.) Just before serving, add the mint and mix gently. Serve immediately, garnished with the peanuts.

braised eggplant with ginger and black beans

3 tablespoons peanut oil

1 tablespoon toasted sesame oil

5 medium Chinese or Italian eggplants, trimmed and cut on the diagonal into 1-inch pieces

5 cloves garlic, finely chopped

5-inch piece fresh ginger root, peeled and thinly sliced

1/2 cup dry sherry or vermouth

3 tablespoons bottled hoisin or plum sauce

2 1/2 tablespoons soy sauce

1 1/2 tablespoons Chinese-style chili–black bean sauce

1 bunch scallions, finely chopped

1/4 cup minced fresh cilantro or sesame seeds, for garnish

➤ To add a delightful crunchy texture to this dish, add about one cup of drained and rinsed water chestnuts along with the scallions. Toss with cooked noodles or serve atop steamed rice. For a cross-cultural salad, serve warm on a bed of mixed baby greens.

All ingredients for this recipe may be purchased in any Asian market and most full-service grocery stores.

HOTTER 6

makes about 4 servings

In a heavy-bottomed shallow saucepan, heat the peanut and sesame oils over moderately high heat until hot but not smoking. Add the eggplant and cook 2 minutes, stirring frequently. Add the garlic and ginger and cook 2 minutes. Add the sherry, hoisin sauce, soy sauce, and chili–black bean sauce and bring to a boil over high heat. Cook 2 minutes, stirring once or twice. Reduce the heat to moderate and cover. Cook 10 to 12 minutes, or until the eggplant is tender but not mushy and the liquids have thickened. Add the scallions and mix gently. Serve immediately, garnished with the cilantro or sesame seeds.

ginger-lemongrass vegetable stir-fry

In a very large, nonstick sauté pan or wok, heat the oil until hot, but not smoking. Add the lemongrass, shallots, garlic, ginger, carrots, and green beans. Cook over high heat 2 minutes, stirring constantly.

Add the lotus root, baby corn, straw mushrooms, fish sauce, sherry, chili paste, and sugar. Cook 2 minutes, stirring constantly, until all vegetables are crisp-tender and sauce is aromatic. Remove from heat. Serve immediately, garnished with the cilantro or basil.

➤ Bright-tasting lemongrass and fresh ginger add sparkle to this colorful Vietnamese stir-fry. For a complete meal, spoon over steamed jasmine rice or toss with cooked noodles.

Asian grocery stores or produce markets and some upscale or natural food stores may carry the ingredients needed for this recipe. If you can't find fresh lotus root, you may use canned instead.

HOTTER 4

makes 4 to 6 servings

2 tablespoons peanut oil

3 stalks lemongrass, trimmed

3 shallots, thinly sliced

3 cloves garlic, finely chopped

4-inch piece fresh ginger root, peeled and thinly sliced

2 medium carrots, slivered

1/2 pound small green beans, trimmed

1/2 fresh lotus root (4 to 5 inches), peeled and thinly sliced

1 can (14 ounces) baby corn or baby bamboo shoots, drained and rinsed

1 can (15 ounces) straw mushrooms, drained and rinsed

3 tablespoons fish sauce (nuoc cham)

2 tablespoons dry sherry

1 1/2 teaspoons Vietnamese or Chinese chili paste

1 teaspoon sugar

1/2 cup finely chopped fresh cilantro or basil, for garnish

ginger-glazed yam cakes with raisins and walnuts

GINGER GLAZE:

2 cups sugar

2 cups water

6-inch piece fresh ginger root, peeled and finely chopped

YAM CAKES:

12 tablespoons (1 1/2 sticks) unsalted butter

1 1/4 cups granulated sugar

1/2 cup dark brown sugar

2 eggs

2 teaspoons vanilla extract

1 1/2 cups cooked, peeled and mashed yams

2 cups cake flour

2 teaspoons baking powder

1 1/2 tablespoons ground cinnamon

1/4 teaspoon kosher or sea salt

1/4 teaspoon ground cloves

3/4 cup sultanas (golden raisins)

3/4 cup coarsely chopped toasted walnuts or pecans

➤ These heavenly little nut- and raisin-studded cakes seem to have a divine effect on all who sample them. This is my favorite baked good; I never tire of their spicy-sweet flavor and moist texture.

HOT 1

makes 8 individual bundt cakes

To make the glaze: In a large, heavy-bottomed saucepan, combine the sugar, water, and ginger. Bring to a boil over moderate heat and cook 10 minutes, stirring occasionally and brushing the sides of the pan from time to time with a pastry brush dipped in cold water. Reduce the heat to moderately low and simmer 30 minutes without stirring, until thick and syrupy.

Remove from the heat and immediately strain through a fine wire mesh or sieve. Cool the syrup to room temperature. Cover with a tight-fitting lid and refrigerate for at least 2 hours before using. (May be refrigerated for up to 1 month.)

To make the Yam Cakes: Generously grease eight, 8-ounce capacity individual bundt pans or jumbo muffin tin cups; set aside. Preheat oven to 400° F.

In a large bowl, cream the butter until very soft. Add the sugars and beat until light and fluffy, about 5 minutes. Add the eggs and vanilla and beat well. Add the yams and mix thoroughly.

In a separate bowl, combine the flour, baking powder, cinnamon, salt, cloves, sultanas, and walnuts; mix thoroughly. Add to the wet ingredients and mix well. Spoon into prepared bundt pans and bake on lower shelf of oven 15 minutes. Reduce oven to 350° F. and rotate pans to upper shelf. Bake 15 to 20 minutes, or until a toothpick inserted into the center of a cake comes out clean. Remove from the oven and cool in pans 5 to 7 minutes. Gently remove cakes and cool on baking racks. When cool, brush with ginger glaze and serve immediately.

Ginger Chicken Salad with Cashew Nuts

GINGER AND MAYONNAISE ARE A SELDOM-SEEN DUO, BUT I FIND THAT THE SHARP, PUNGENT, SLIGHTLY SWEET TASTE OF FRESH GINGER ROOT PLEASINGLY OFFSETS THE RICH QUALITY OF MAYONNAISE AND CASHEW NUTS IN THIS DISTINCTIVE SALAD. **MAKES 4 TO 6 SERVINGS. ∽ HOT #1**

4 chicken breast halves

6-inch piece fresh ginger root, coarsely chopped

1 large bunch scallions, trimmed and finely chopped

1 cup water chestnuts, halved

5-inch piece fresh ginger root, peeled and
  finely chopped

1¼ cups mayonnaise (preferably homemade)

¼ cup fresh lemon juice

Salt and pepper, to taste

1 cup roasted cashews

Watercress, for lining platter

In a 6-quart pot, place the chicken breasts, 4 quarts of cold water, and the coarsely chopped ginger. Bring to a boil over high heat. Using a slotted spoon, remove the foam from the surface and discard. Reduce the heat to moderately low and cook approximately 15 minutes, until the chicken is opaque in the center. Take care not to overcook the chicken. Drain in a colander and cool the chicken to room temperature.

When cool enough to handle, keeping the breast meat intact, remove the skin, bones, tendons, cartilage, and fat; discard. Cut the chicken into ½-inch chunks and place in a large bowl along with the scallions, water chestnuts, finely chopped ginger, mayonnaise, and lemon juice. Mix gently and season with salt and pepper. Serve immediately or store in a tightly sealed container in the refrigerator for up to 3 days. Just before serving, add the cashews and mix well. Serve on a platter covered with watercress.

1 pound filet mignon steaks, trimmed of fat

4 cloves garlic, thinly sliced

4-inch piece ginger root, peeled and minced

2 tablespoons *nuoc cham* (fish sauce)

2 tablespoons soy sauce

1 tablespoon sugar

Dressing:

½ cup peanut oil

¼ cup fresh lime juice

1 small red onion, halved and thinly sliced

3 cloves garlic, minced

3-inch piece ginger root, peeled and slivered

1 to 2 red or green jalapeño peppers, stemmed, cut in thin rounds

Salt and pepper, to taste

1 small head butter lettuce, leaves separated

½ cup chopped cilantro, for garnish

½ cup mint leaves, for garnish

Warm Thai Ginger Beef Salad

This classic Thai beef salad is served barely warm, and is delicious for lunch or a light supper with fried noodles or steamed rice. Icy cold Thai beer would be a good accompaniment to this spicy, flavorful Southeast Asian dish.
Makes 4 servings. *Hotter: rated 6*

Place the steaks in a nonreactive bowl with the garlic, ginger, *nuoc cham*, and soy sauce, and the sugar; mix well and let stand at room temperature for 30 minutes to 1 hour.

To make the dressing: Place 6 tablespoons of the peanut oil in a small bowl. Using a wire whisk, incorporate the lime juice a little at a time, whisking all the while to form a smooth emulsion. Add the onion, garlic, ginger, and jalapeño pepper; mix well. Season with salt and pepper and set aside until needed.

Heat the remaining 2 tablespoons of peanut oil in a wok or a large nonstick sauté pan over high heat. When the oil is hot, add the steaks along with some of the bits of ginger and garlic, and cook over moderately high heat for 2 to 3 minutes per side. Remove from the pan and cool slightly.

Cut the steaks into ¼-inch thick slices and add to the dressing. Mix well and arrange the dressed beef on beds of butter lettuce. Garnish with the cilantro and mint, and serve immediately.

Tuna Tartare with Ginger

Ruby red and jewel-like, a Japanese-style tuna dish makes a stunning appetizer, but it is also good served with sautéed vegetables for a light supper in hot weather. Be sure to get fresh tuna from your fishmonger, as it is eaten uncooked, sushi style. Makes 4 to 6 servings.   *Hot: rated 3*

Using a very sharp cleaver or knife, mince the tuna by hand, rather than in a food processor. (The texture of very fresh fish is important to the dish's appeal, and cutting with a knife by hand is the best way to achieve the desired texture.) Place the tuna in a glass or plastic bowl.

Add the sesame oil, sherry, vinegar, chives, and ginger; mix well. Taste and season with salt and black pepper if needed. Refrigerate until ready to serve, but is best eaten right away. Arrange on a bed of greens and garnish with the sesame seeds and optionally, chive blossoms.

1½ pounds lean, fresh tuna fillet

2 tablespoons Asian sesame oil

2 tablespoons dry sherry or mirin (sweet rice wine)

1 tablespoon seasoned rice wine vinegar

½ cup minced chives

4-inch piece ginger root, peeled and slivered

Salt and pepper, to taste

Mixed greens: baby mustard greens, or rocket, mizuna, or baby lettuces

¼ cup black sesame seeds, for garnish

Chive blossoms, for garnish (optional)

Burmese Prawn Salad with Fried Shallots and Ginger

CHARACTERISTIC OF MANY SOUTHEAST ASIAN DISHES, THIS PALATE-AWAKENING SALAD DEPENDS ON A VARIETY
OF CONTRASTING INGREDIENTS FOR ITS STIMULATING TEXTURE AND FLAVOR.

MAKES 6 SERVINGS. ⌒ HOT #2

¾ pound small prawns

5 tablespoons peanut oil

4 large shallots, halved and thinly sliced

4-inch piece fresh ginger root, peeled and
  finely chopped

2 tablespoons light soy sauce

2 tablespoons fresh lime juice

1 tablespoon fish sauce (Nuoc Cham)

3-inch piece fresh ginger root, peeled and minced

2 cloves garlic, minced

2½ cups finely shredded white cabbage

1 medium onion, halved and thinly sliced

⅓ cup finely chopped fresh cilantro, for garnish

Bring 2 quarts of water to boil in a large saucepan. Add the prawns, stir well, and cook 1 minute. Immediately drain in a colander and refresh with cold water. Transfer to a bowl filled with cold water and let stand 5 minutes. Drain well. Peel the prawns and remove tails; set aside until needed.

In a medium sauté pan, heat 3 tablespoons of the peanut oil over moderately high heat. When the oil is hot but not smoking, add the shallots and cook 4 minutes, stirring constantly, until they are golden brown and crisp. Add the finely chopped ginger and cook 2 or 3 minutes. Remove from the pan and drain on paper towels. Set aside until needed.

In a large bowl, combine the remaining 2 tablespoons peanut oil with the soy sauce, whisking constantly with a wire whisk to form a smooth emulsion. Add the lime juice, fish sauce, minced ginger and garlic; mix well. Add the cabbage, onion, and half of the prawns; toss gently. Arrange on a large platter, top with the remaining prawns, and garnish with the fried shallot-ginger mixture and the cilantro. Serve immediately.

Sizzling Prawns with Ginger

This Chinese-style stir-fry dish is easy to prepare. You may increase the Chinese hot chili paste to suit your taste, but I suggest you sample the paste before you add it to the entire dish—some commercial chili pastes are extremely hot, while others are quite tame in comparison. Serve this colorful, light dinner or lunch dish with steamed rice, fried noodles, or on a bed of mixed greens for a cross-cultural meal.

Makes 4 to 6 servings.   *Hottest: rated 8*

3 tablespoons peanut oil

1 pound medium-sized prawns, peeled and tails removed

1 large red bell pepper, cut in julienne

4-inch piece ginger root, peeled and finely chopped

4 cloves garlic, thinly sliced

1 teaspoon Chinese hot chili paste

2 tablespoons dry sherry

1 small bunch green onions, trimmed, cut in 1-inch pieces

¼ cup soy sauce

¾ cup toasted peanuts

¾ cup chopped cilantro

Heat a very large nonstick sauté pan or a large wok over high heat until it is hot. Add the oil and heat until it just begins to smoke. Add the prawns, red bell pepper, ginger, garlic, chili paste, and sherry, and cook over high heat for 1 minute, stirring all the while. Add the onions, soy sauce, and peanuts and cook for 1 minute, stirring constantly. Add half of the cilantro and mix well.

Turn the prawns onto a large platter, garnish with the remaining cilantro, and serve immediately with steamed rice or noodles.

Hunan Scallops with Black Beans and Ginger-Chili Oil

Ginger-Chili Oil:

½ cup peanut oil

4 dried red chilies, crushed

4-inch piece ginger root, peeled and minced

2 cloves garlic, thinly sliced

2 tablespoons Asian sesame oil

2 tablespoons soy sauce

2 tablespoons peanut oil

4-inch piece ginger root, peeled and slivered

1 pound scallops, muscles removed

3 tablespoons preserved black beans

3 tablespoons dry sherry

1 large red bell pepper, cut in julienne

2 cups fresh spinach leaves

Hunan-style Chinese cuisine is characterized in part by the abundance of ginger, garlic, and hot chilies. This fiery seafood dish is beautiful served on a bed of spinach or shredded green cabbage, or served with steamed rice for a more traditional meal.
Makes 4 servings.   *Hotter: rated 6*

To make the Ginger-Chili Oil: In a heavy-bottomed skillet, heat the peanut oil, chilies, ginger, and garlic over moderate heat, stirring constantly for 2 minutes, until it begins to sizzle. Add the sesame oil and soy sauce and cook for 2 minutes. Remove from the heat and cool slightly. Strain through a fine wire mesh and set aside until needed.

A scant 5 minutes before you want to serve the scallops, heat the peanut oil in a wok or very large nonstick sauté pan over high heat. When the oil is very hot, add the ginger and scallops. Cook for 2 minutes, stirring all the while. Add the black beans, sherry, and red bell pepper, and cook for 1 more minute, stirring constantly. Remove from the heat and arrange on top of the spinach leaves. Drizzle with the Ginger-Chili Oil and serve immediately.

Grilled Ginger-Orange Chicken with Ginger Sauce

Marinade:

1½ cups peanut oil

½ cup orange juice

¼ cup soy sauce

¾ cup honey

12-inch piece ginger root, peeled and minced

⅓ cup ground ginger powder

2 tablespoons ground coriander

1 large chicken plus 2 legs (about 4 pounds), cut into serving pieces

Sauce:

½ cup corn syrup

3 tablespoons rice wine vinegar

3 tablespoons fresh lime juice

2 cloves garlic, finely chopped

4-inch piece ginger root, peeled and finely chopped

Salt and pepper, to taste

Cilantro sprigs, for garnish

Most all Asian-style marinades are wonderful with chicken or turkey, as they are aromatic and flavorful but don't overpower the delicate flavors of the meat. Basmati rice or noodles served along with a green vegetable would make this a complete and simple dinner.
Makes 4 to 6 servings.   *Hot: rated 3*

To make the marinade: Place the olive oil in a bowl. Slowly add the orange juice, whisking all the while to make a smooth emulsion. Slowly add the soy sauce and honey, whisking all the while. Add the ginger and coriander; mix well.

Arrange the chicken in a shallow nonreactive vessel and pour the marinade over it. You may use a plastic bag for this (be sure to leave it in a container in case the bag leaks). Marinate for 1 to 2 days in the refrigerator, rotating the chicken so that the marinade comes in contact with the meat at all times.

To make the sauce: Combine all the ingredients except the cilantro in a nonreactive bowl; mix well and season with salt and pepper.

Prepare a charcoal grill. When the coals are medium hot (a light layer of gray ash will cover the coals), place the chicken on the grill skin side down. Cook the chicken, rotating it to prevent it from burning, for 35 to 40 minutes, or until it is dark brown and the meat is cooked all the way to the bone. The cooking time will vary according to the heat of your fire. Remove the chicken and let stand at room temperature for 5 minutes before serving. Garnish with cilantro and serve with the sauce.

Chinese Stir-Fried Beef with Ginger

TO FACILITATE SLICING THE BEEF, WRAP IT IN PLASTIC AND PLACE IN THE FREEZER FOR THIRTY MINUTES PRIOR TO CUTTING. THIS CLASSIC CHINESE DISH IS BEST SERVED WITH A LARGE BOWL OF STEAMED RICE OR WITH COOKED CHINESE NOODLES.

MAKES ABOUT 4 SERVINGS. ∽HOT #3

In a nonreactive bowl, combine the beef, soy sauce, sherry, vinegar, white pepper, sugar, and garlic; mix well and let stand at room temperature for 30 to 40 minutes. Using your fingers, lift the meat from the bowl and gently squeeze the excess liquid from the meat back into the bowl. Add the cornstarch, oyster sauce, and chicken broth to the liquid and mix well; set aside.

In a very large, nonstick sauté pan or wok, heat the oil over high heat until it just begins to smoke. Immediately add the meat and ginger and cook 30 seconds, stirring constantly. Add the corn-starch mixture and the scallions and cook 1½ minutes, stirring constantly, until the sauce is thick and aromatic. Remove from the pan and serve immediately, garnished with the sesame seeds.

1 pound beef flank steak, cut across the grain into slices about 1½ inches long and ⅛ inch thick

¼ cup soy sauce

¼ cup dry sherry

¼ cup rice wine vinegar

2 teaspoons white pepper

1 teaspoon sugar

3 cloves garlic, finely chopped

2 teaspoons cornstarch

1½ tablespoons oyster sauce

⅔ cup low-sodium chicken broth or water

2 tablespoons peanut oil

4½-inch piece fresh ginger root, peeled and slivered

6 scallions, trimmed and sliced into 1-inch pieces

1½ tablespoons sesame seeds, for garnish

Cold Noodles with Asian Vegetables and Ginger Peanut Sauce

PRESENTED AS A LIGHT SUPPER OR A COMPLETE LUNCH, THIS COLORFUL AND HEALTHFUL ROOM-TEMPERATURE SALAD IS TERRIFIC DURING THE WARM-WEATHER MONTHS.

MAKES 4 TO 6 SERVINGS. ⁓HOT #3

Bring 3 quarts of salted water to boil in a 6-quart pot. Add the noodles and cook 6 to 7 minutes, or until they are al dente. Drain in a colander and refresh with cold water. Spread the noodles on kitchen towels or on layers of paper towels and pat dry. Transfer to a large bowl and add the bell pepper, snow peas, scallions, and cilantro. Set aside.

To MAKE THE GINGER PEANUT SAUCE: In a medium bowl, combine the peanut and sesame oils. Slowly add the lime juice, whisking constantly with a wire whisk to form a smooth emulsion. Slowly add the soy sauce, whisking constantly. Add the ginger, garlic, and chilies and mix well. Season with salt and pepper.

Add three fourths of the ginger peanut sauce and three fourths of the peanuts to the noodle-vegetable mixture; toss gently. Mound the salad in the center of a large platter. Arrange the cucumbers around the edge of the salad. Drizzle with the remaining sauce and garnish with the remaining peanuts. Serve immediately.

¾ pound round Chinese egg noodles
   (preferably fresh)
1 small red bell pepper, stemmed, seeded, and slivered
¼ pound snow peas, blanched, trimmed,
   and thinly sliced lengthwise
4 scallions, trimmed and finely chopped
½ cup finely chopped fresh cilantro

GINGER PEANUT SAUCE:
1 cup peanut oil
1 tablespoon sesame oil
3 tablespoons fresh lime juice
2 tablespoons light soy sauce
4-inch piece fresh ginger root, peeled and minced
3 cloves garlic, minced
2 serrano chili peppers, stemmed and thinly sliced
Salt and pepper, to taste

¾ cup finely chopped roasted peanuts
½ English cucumber, thinly sliced

Eggplant Ravioli with Ginger-Cilantro Sauce

A blend of Italian and Asian ingredients and cooking methods make this a whimsical cross-cultural dish. Mediterranean herbs, eggplant, vinegar, and nuts form a robust filling, but the delicate Asian wonton wrappers and barely thickened sauce lend a refined texture and elegance to these raviolis.
Makes 4 to 6 servings (24 raviolis)   *Hotter: rated 4*

To make the sauce: Place the chicken stock and ginger in a large pan. Bring to a boil over high heat. Cook over high heat for 5 minutes. Combine the cornstarch and sherry in a small bowl; mix well. Slowly add this "slurry" to the chicken stock, stirring as you go. Continue boiling until the mixture starts to thicken. Reduce the heat and cook for 10 minutes over moderate heat. (You will add the red pepper flakes and cilantro just before serving.)

To make the filling: Cook the onion, garlic, and herbs in the olive oil over moderate heat for 15 minutes, stirring from time to time. Add the ginger and eggplant and cook over high heat for 5 minutes, stirring constantly. Add the vinegar and cook over moderate heat for 5 to 7 minutes, stirring frequently, until the eggplant is soft and tender. Add the pine nuts and tomato paste, mix well, and season with salt and pepper. Cool to room temperature.

To make the raviolis: Combine the cornstarch with the water in a small bowl. Arrange 10 skins on a flat surface. Lightly brush each skin with the slurry. Place 1½ to 2 teaspoons of filling in the center of each skin. Cover with a second skin, pressing the two sides together from the filling out to the edge of the skin, removing any air bubbles as you secure the two skins. Place on a sheet pan and continue making the raviolis until all the filling is used up. Refrigerate for up to 1 hour before cooking.

The skins become a bit soggy if they are stored in the refrigerator for longer than one hour. If you can't cook the raviolis within that time, freeze them on a sheet pan. When they are completely frozen, place the raviolis in a bag and store in the freezer until you are ready to cook.

Sauce:

1 quart chicken stock

4-inch piece ginger root, peeled and slivered

2 tablespoons cornstarch

½ cup dry sherry

1 teaspoon dried red pepper flakes

1 cup chopped cilantro

Filling:

1 large onion, cut in small dice

3 cloves garlic, minced

2 teaspoons each dried rosemary and thyme and ground coriander

⅓ cup olive oil

6-inch piece ginger root, peeled and minced

3 medium Japanese or Italian eggplants, cut in small dice

¼ cup balsamic vinegar

½ cup toasted pine nuts

3 tablespoons tomato paste

Salt and pepper, to taste

1 package potsticker or gyoza
skins (about 60 skins)

¼ cup cornstarch

1 cup water

To cook the raviolis: Bring a large pot of salted water to boil over high heat. When the water is boiling, add a batch and cook for 3 to 4 minutes (6 to 7 minutes if frozen), or until they are tender and the skins are transparent all the way through. Remove with a slotted spoon and drain in a colander. (The raviolis will stick together if you let them sit in the colander for more than a couple of minutes. If this happens, place the clump in a bowl of warm water and carefully separate with your fingers.)

Immediately place the raviolis in shallow bowls. Add some of the red pepper flakes and cilantro to each bowl and drizzle with some of the sauce.

Poached Nectarines with Ginger and Crème Fraîche

2 cups water

2 cups fruity white wine

2 cups sugar

4-inch piece ginger root, peeled and thinly sliced

6 ripe but firm nectarines, quartered and pits removed

1 teaspoon almond extract

1 cup crème fraîche (or sour cream thinned with a little water)

¼ cup candied ginger, slivered

Mint sprigs, for garnish

Spicy yet refreshing, this fruit concoction is a wonderful warm-weather dessert. Use apricots, peaches, or even peeled oranges in combination with the nectarines if you like. When the ginger cooks in the sweet liquid the slices curl in a most delightful way, and add texture and intriguing shapes to this fruit dessert.
Makes 4 to 6 servings   *Hot: rated 3*

Place the water, wine, sugar, and ginger in a heavy-bottomed saucepan. Bring to a boil over high heat and cook for 20 minutes, stirring frequently. Add the nectarines, reduce the heat to moderately low, and cook until the fruit is tender but not mushy, 2 to 3 minutes. Remove from the heat and add the almond extract.

Serve warm or at room temperature in a little of the cooking liquid and a drizzle of crème fraîche, topped with a few slivers of candied ginger and sprigs of mint.

Spiced Indian Cauliflower with Ginger

If you would like to make this a true vegetarian dish, omit the chicken stock and use a light tomato or vegetable broth instead. This spicy Indian vegetable dish is excellent with lamb, chicken, or beef dishes, and also goes well with stewed lentils and Indian breads.
Makes 4 to 6 servings.   *Hotter: rated 6*

Place the ginger, garlic, spices, olive oil, and ½ cup of the chicken stock in a blender. Purée until fairly smooth. Remove from the blender.

Heat a deep-sided, nonstick skillet large enough to accommodate all the cauliflower. Over high heat, cook the ginger paste and cauliflower, stirring constantly, for 1 minute. Add the remaining chicken stock and bring to a boil still over high heat.

Reduce the heat to moderate and cook, uncovered, until the cauliflower is almost tender—7 to 8 minutes, or until almost all the liquid has evaporated. Add the lemon juice, red pepper, and cilantro and cook for 3 to 4 minutes. Season with salt and pepper, mix well, and serve immediately.

4-inch piece ginger root, peeled and coarsely chopped

3 cloves garlic

1 tablespoon ground coriander

1 teaspoon each ground turmeric, mace, cayenne, and cumin

¼ cup olive oil

2 cups chicken stock

8 cups or 3 small heads cauliflower, cut in 1-inch flowerettes

Juice from 2 lemons

1 large red bell pepper, cut in small dice

1 cup chopped cilantro

Salt and pepper, to taste

Apricot-Ginger Chutney

AT ONCE TART, SWEET, AND SPICY, THIS CHUTNEY IS AN EXCELLENT COMPANION TO POULTRY OR PORK,
OR TO SHARP CHEDDAR CHEESE AND CRACKERS.
MAKES ABOUT 2¼ CUPS. ∽ HOT #3

1 medium red onion, cut into small dice

2 cloves garlic, finely chopped

2 tablespoons peanut oil

*½ teaspoon each ground cardamom, coriander,
fennel seeds, anise, and fenugreek*

½ cup water

*5-inch piece fresh ginger root, peeled and
finely chopped*

6 large apricots, pitted and coarsely chopped

⅓ cup fresh lemon juice

Salt and pepper, to taste

In a large, shallow saucepan, cook the onion and garlic in the peanut oil over moderate heat for 5 minutes, stirring frequently. Add the spices and cook 2 minutes, stirring constantly. Add the water and cook 5 to 7 minutes, or until it has evaporated. Add the ginger, apricots, and lemon juice and cook 15 to 20 minutes, stirring occasionally, until the mixture is thick and aromatic. Season with salt and pepper. Store in a tightly sealed container in the refrigerator for up to 10 days.

Spiced Ginger Cake with Candied Ginger Cream

THIS MOIST, LIGHTLY SWEETENED CAKE IS REDOLENT OF FRESH GINGER AND SPICES, MAKING IT IDEAL FOR SERVING FOR BRUNCH OR AS A REFRESHING ALTERNATIVE TO A RICH, HEAVY AFTER-DINNER DESSERT.

Candied ginger is available at specialty food stores, gourmet food shops, and most candy stores; however, Asian grocery stores usually sell this delicacy for half the price.

MAKES 9 TO 12 SERVINGS. ∼ **HOT #2**

Preheat oven to 350° F. Generously grease and lightly flour a 10 by-13-inch baking pan.

TO MAKE THE CAKE: In a large bowl, using an electric mixer, beat the sugar and vegetable oil together until pale and smooth, about 3 or 4 minutes. Add the eggs one at a time, beating well after each addition. Add the carrots and ginger and mix well.

Combine the dry ingredients, including the nuts, in a medium bowl; mix well. Add to the egg mixture and mix just until combined. Pour the batter into the prepared pan and bake on the lower rack of the oven for 30 minutes. Rotate to the upper shelf and bake 20 to 25 minutes longer, or until a toothpick inserted into the center of the cake comes out clean. Remove from the oven and cool to room temperature. Run a dull knife around the edges of the cake and cut into serving pieces.

TO MAKE THE CANDIED GINGER CREAM: Place the cream in a medium bowl. Using an electric mixer, beat on high speed until soft peaks form. Add the sugar and liqueur and beat until firm enough to hold its shape but not stiff. Add the finely chopped candied ginger and mix gently.

Spread the top of each piece with some of the Candied Ginger Cream and serve garnished with the sliced candied ginger and mint sprigs.

SPICED GINGER CAKE:

2 cups granulated sugar

1½ cups vegetable oil

4 eggs, lightly beaten

1½ cups finely grated carrots

1½ cups minced peeled fresh ginger root

2 cups all-purpose flour

2 teaspoons baking powder

1½ teaspoons baking soda

1 teaspoon salt

2½ tablespoons ground ginger powder

2½ teaspoons each ground cinnamon and mace

1½ cups coarsely chopped toasted walnuts

CANDIED GINGER CREAM:

1½ cups heavy cream

⅓ cup sifted powdered sugar

1 tablespoon ginger liqueur or light rum

1 cup finely chopped candied ginger

Mint sprigs and thinly sliced candied ginger, for garnish

Apple, Ginger, and Mint Sorbet

THIS IS ONE OF MY ALL-TIME FAVORITE FLAVOR COMBINATIONS, SIMULTANEOUSLY FIERY, ICY, AND REFRESHING.
SERVE THIS SORBET AS A PALATE CLEANSER BETWEEN COURSES OR AS AN INVIGORATING DESSERT AFTER A RICH MEAL.
MAKES 6 TO 8 SERVINGS. ⌒ HOTTER #4

3 cups water

3 cups sugar

5-inch piece fresh ginger root, coarsely chopped

*1 cup firmly packed, coarsely chopped fresh
    mint leaves*

*2 large tart green apples, peeled, cored, and
    finely chopped*

⅓ cup fresh lemon juice

*2-inch piece fresh ginger root, peeled and
    finely chopped*

20 ice cubes, coarsely crushed

Mint sprigs, for garnish

In a 6-quart heavy-bottomed saucepan, combine the water, sugar, coarsely chopped ginger, and mint. Bring to a boil over high heat, stirring constantly. Boil for 35 to 40 minutes, stirring frequently to prevent the mixture from boiling over, until the mixture is thick and syrupy. Remove from the heat and strain through a fine wire sieve.

Return the syrup to the saucepan and bring to a boil over high heat; cook 3 minutes, stirring constantly. Add the apples and lemon juice and cook 3 to 4 minutes, or until the apples are just tender. Remove from the heat and cool slightly. Add the finely chopped ginger and mix well.

In a blender, puree the mixture until smooth, stopping occasionally to scrape the sides of the container. Transfer to a nonreactive container and freeze for at least 6 hours or up to 2 days. (The mixture won't freeze solid, but it will become slushy.)

Before serving, place half of the ice cubes and half of the fruit mixture in the blender. Blend until the ice is finely crushed and the mixture is smooth and icy. (If you're only serving three or four people, stop at this point and reserve the other half for later.) Blend the remaining ice cubes and fruit mixture. Serve immediately, garnished with sprigs of fresh mint.

bittersweet chocolate ginger coins

To make crystallized ginger: In a 6-quart, heavy-bottomed saucepan, place the ginger and 2 quarts of cold water. Bring to a boil over high heat. Remove from heat and cool to room temperature. Drain well.

Return the ginger to the pan and add 2 quarts of fresh cold water. Add 2 cups of the granulated sugar and bring to a boil over moderate heat. Reduce heat and simmer 15 minutes. Cool to room temperature, cover, and let stand 8 hours or overnight.

Add 2 more cups of the granulated sugar and 1 cup of the corn syrup to the pan. Cover and bring to a boil over moderate heat; boil 5 minutes. Remove the cover and cook 20 minutes, stirring occasionally. Replace the cover, remove from the heat, and cool to room temperature. Let stand 8 hours or overnight.

Add the remaining 1 cup *each* granulated sugar and corn syrup; mix well. Bring to a boil over moderate heat. Boil 25 to 35 minutes, or until the ginger is tender and translucent. Remove from the heat, cover, and cool to room temperature. Using a slotted spoon, remove the ginger from the syrup and drain on baking racks overnight.

Place the 1½ cups castor or granulated sugar in a large bowl. Add the ginger and mix well using your fingers; take care to separate the ginger and coat each piece evenly with the sugar. Arrange the ginger in a single layer on a baking sheet.

To make the chocolate coins: Heat the chocolate in the top of a double boiler over moderately low heat until just melted. Using a spoon, drizzle the chocolate over the ginger to make fine stripes. When the chocolate is cool and firm, remove ginger and store in a tightly sealed box at room temperature for up to 1 month (several months without the chocolate).

➤ This recipe begins with directions for making crystallized ginger, which is then drizzled with bittersweet chocolate to make a sensational confection. Although you can purchase crystallized ginger ready-made, it's much more gratifying and fun to make it yourself. As a bonus, you end up with a super-concentrated ginger-flavored syrup you can add to iced beverages and hot tea, drizzle over ice cream or frozen yogurt, and use in all sorts of desserts. And once you see how easy the crystallizing process is, you'll be turning all kinds of fresh fruit into sugared jewels.

Be sure to use fat, round ginger roots with as few knobs as possible.

HOTTER 6

makes about 2½ cups ginger coins

12-inch section fresh ginger root, knobs removed, peeled and cut on the diagonal into ¼-inch-thick discs (about 2½ cups)

5 cups granulated sugar

2 cups corn syrup

1½ cups golden castor or granulated sugar, for coating

4 ounces bittersweet chocolate

Pickled Ginger

FOR A TRADITIONAL PRESENTATION, PAIR THIS INVIGORATING CONDIMENT WITH SUSHI OR SASHIMI.
FOR LESS CONVENTIONAL APPLICATIONS, BRIGHTEN THE FLAVOR OF SAUTÉED POULTRY, FISH, SEAFOOD, OR MEAT DISHES,
OR VEGETABLE, PASTA OR RICE SALADS BY ADDING THE PICKLED SLICES WHOLE OR FINELY CHOPPED.
MAKES 2 CUPS. ∽ HOT #6

*When making pickled ginger, look for young ginger in Asian grocery stores and produce markets.
If you cannot locate this tender, juicy variety, use regular ginger and peel before slicing.*

Arrange the sliced ginger in a single layer in a large, nonreactive baking pan. Sprinkle with the salt and cover with plastic wrap. Let sit overnight at room temperature. Transfer to a glass container large enough to accommodate the remaining ingredients. Add the vinegar and sugar; cover tightly and shake vigorously to combine the ingredients. Refrigerate for at least 1 week before serving. The ginger will keep for up to 3 months if stored in the refrigerator. Drain slightly before serving.

1 pound fresh young ginger root, sliced crosswise into paper-thin rounds

1½ tablespoons kosher salt

1 cup rice wine vinegar or white wine vinegar

3 tablespoons sugar

frozen ginger-peach yogurt with cinnamon

2 cups vanilla low-fat yogurt

1 jar (7 ounces) marshmallow cream

3 large peaches, pitted and finely chopped

5-inch piece fresh ginger root, peeled and minced

1 tablespoon ground cinnamon

Fresh mint sprigs and/or ¼ cup finely chopped toasted almonds, for garnish

➤ You may never eat store-bought ice cream or frozen yogurt again after tasting the homemade version that follows. This summery, low-fat dessert can be frozen in a covered container in your freezer—you don't need an ice-cream maker for this treat.

HOTTER 4

makes about 6 servings

In a large bowl, whisk together 1 cup of the yogurt with the marshmallow cream until thoroughly combined. Add the remaining yogurt and mix until smooth. Add the peaches, ginger, and cinnamon and mix well. Transfer to a shallow, flat-bottomed plastic or stainless steel container and cover with a tight-fitting lid. Place in the freezer for 1 hour. Remove and stir vigorously with a fork. Return to the freezer and mix again in 2 hours. Return to the freezer and freeze until firm.

To present free-form in bowls, remove from the freezer 10 to 15 minutes prior to serving to soften slightly before spooning into small bowls. To serve in square or rectangular shapes on dessert plates, remove from the freezer and cut into the desired shapes. Serve immediately, garnished with mint sprigs and/or finely chopped toasted almonds.

horseradish

HORSERADISH

FEW FOODS COME CLOSE TO THE POWER AND INTENSITY OF FRESHLY GRATED HORSERADISH. Once peeled and grated, a fresh root emits a vapor so potent it could penetrate a cement wall.

A member of the *Cruciferae* family, horseradish is a perennial plant native to eastern Europe and western Asia. It now grows in Britain, Russia, northern Europe, and the United States. The plant has long, dark green leaves that can be used in salads and other savory dishes, but it is the root that appears most frequently in prepared foods and condiments.

Approximately the size of a half-dollar in circumference, the ten- to twelve-inch-long root is rough and knobby, with pale yellow to light brown skin tone and ivory-colored, slightly fibrous flesh. Fresh roots must be carefully washed with warm water and a vegetable brush to remove caked-on dirt. Once cleaned, use a sharp paring knife to remove the thin outer skin. At this point you can either grate, finely mince, dice, julienne, or coarsely chop the root.

When buying fresh horseradish, look for hard, relatively unblemished roots that do not yield to bending motions (rubbery roots are past their prime and short on flavor). To store fresh horseradish, loosely wrap in paper towels, place inside a plastic bag, and store in the refrigerator for up to one and a half months. Some people prefer storing the root inside a paper bag, but I feel the additional plastic wrapping provides better insulation. Depending on how fresh the root was when purchased, horseradish can keep for up to three months in the refrigerator. Once opened, prepared commercial horseradish loses potency. Store the condiment in the refrigerator for up to four or five months.

To GRATE HORSERADISH: As called for in recipes that follow, use the finest setting of the grater.

To FINELY MINCE HORSERADISH: Slice the root into very thin rounds. Spread the slices on a cutting board, and using a sharp chef's knife or a cleaver, chop into tiny pieces no larger than 1/16 inch.

To COARSELY CHOP HORSERADISH: Follow the same instructions as for finely mincing but chop into rough-sized pieces about ¼ inch in size.

To DICE HORSERADISH: Cut the root into 2- or 3-inch lengths. Depending on the size of the dice (thinner slices for small dice and thicker for large dice), cut the root from top to bottom into long slices. Using three or four slices, make a neat stack. Cut the pieces lengthwise into the desired width, then cut across the thin strips to form the desired-size dice.

To JULIENNE HORSERADISH: Follow the instructions for dicing but omit the last step—simply cut the slices into the desired width, but do not cut across into square dice shapes.

These recipes call for the fresh root in inch lengths, but since roots vary slightly in size, it is impossible to obtain exact measurements for recipes. As with ginger root, precision is not critical. Although I have suggested quantities, adjust the amounts of horseradish called for in recipes to suit your personal taste.

1- TO 2-INCH PIECE FRESH HORSERADISH ROOT = ABOUT ¼ CUP GRATED

2- TO 3-INCH PIECE FRESH HORSERADISH ROOT = ABOUT ½ CUP GRATED

5- TO 6-INCH PIECE FRESH HORSERADISH ROOT = ABOUT 1 CUP GRATED

Fresh horseradish root imparts the greatest essence when grated. It lends a generous amount of flavor when finely minced, and a moderate quantity when diced or coarsely chopped. Like many fresh ingredients, horseradish is most potent in its raw form. Retaining a moderate amount of flavor when heated, fresh horseradish root and prepared horseradish lose most of their intensity when cooked for extended periods of time. For this reason, add the ingredient toward the end of cooking for a pronounced flavor, or after a dish has completely cooled for the most dramatic effect.

The recipes that follow range from mild to scorching; some are saturated with the essence of horseradish while others only hint of it. Strongly infused with the flavor of fresh horseradish are the *New Potato Salad with Sour Cream–Horseradish Dressing* and the *Smoked Ham and Cabbage Slaw with Horseradish*—both are outstanding salads that taste best when served at cool room temperature. *The Roast Beef and Vegetable Rolls with Horseradish Cream Cheese* and the delectable *Pork Tenderloin and Cucumber Sandwiches with Horseradish Mayonnaise* highlight the sinus-clearing qualities of freshly grated horseradish, while the *Green Bean Salad with Creamy Almond-Horseradish Dressing* features the root as a more subtle flavoring agent.

Remember, when preparing fresh horseradish, open the window closest to your work area to allow exit for the pungent fumes. As the recipes in this chapter hopefully will demonstrate, the heady effects and distinctive flavor of fresh horseradish are worth a few tears.

1 cup catsup or cocktail sauce

2- to 3-inch piece horseradish root, peeled and grated

1 clove garlic, minced

3 tablespoons fresh lemon juice

½ teaspoon celery seed

Dash Tabasco sauce

Salt and pepper, to taste

1 pound large prawns

3 tablespoons minced parsley, for garnish

Classic Shrimp Cocktail

There isn't much to improve on when it comes to this classic American appetizer. Fresh horseradish, rather than prepared, adds depth and more zing to this already pungent red sauce. You can serve the seafood on a bed of shredded cabbage, greens, or in the traditional shrimp cocktail glass. An ice cold beer is the perfect beverage with this dish.
Makes 4 servings.   *Hottest: rated 8*

In a nonreactive bowl, combine the catsup, horseradish, garlic, lemon juice, celery seed, Tabasco sauce, and salt and pepper; mix well. This will keep in the refrigerator for up to 2 weeks.

Bring a large pot of water to boil over high heat. When the water is boiling, add the prawns and stir. Cook for 1 to 1½ minutes, or until the prawns are brightly colored and cooked through. Do not overcook the prawns. Drain and rinse with cold water.

When the prawns are cool enough to handle, remove the shells and tails. Combine with the cocktail sauce and refrigerate for 1 hour, or arrange the prawns around a bowl of the sauce. Serve chilled, with chopped parsley for a garnish.

Pan-Fried Potato and Horseradish Cakes

IF YOU LIKE TO START YOUR DAY WITH FOODS MORE FLAVORFUL THAN CEREAL OR PASTRY, TRY THESE
GOLDEN BROWN POTATO CAKES LACED WITH FRESH HORSERADISH. FOR A COMPLETE BREAKFAST, PAIR WITH EGGS AND
SMOKED HAM OR SAUSAGES AND PERHAPS A BASKET OF TOASTED BREAD.

MAKES 16 CAKES; 6 TO 8 SERVINGS. ~ HOT #3

4 large baking potatoes, peeled and quartered

2 large onions, cut into small dice

2 tablespoons olive oil

2 tablespoons unsalted butter

½ cup dry sherry

6 scallions, trimmed and minced

6-inch piece fresh horseradish root, peeled and coarsely grated

3 tablespoons sour cream, plus additional for drizzling (optional)

Salt and pepper, to taste

2 eggs, lightly beaten

1 cup finely ground bread crumbs

¾ to 1 cup vegetable oil, for cooking

Place the potatoes and 3 quarts of salted water in a large pot. Bring to a boil over high heat. Reduce the heat to moderate and cook about 15 minutes, or until the potatoes are tender but not mushy. Drain well in a colander and place in a large bowl. Using a hand-held potato masher, mash the potatoes to a fine consistency. Set aside until needed.

In a very large sauté pan, cook the onions in the olive oil and butter over high heat for 10 minutes, stirring frequently, until light golden brown. Add the sherry and cook 1 minute. Reduce the heat to moderately low and cook 20 minutes, or until the onions are dark brown, very soft, and sweet. Add the scallions and cook 30 seconds. Add to the potatoes along with the horseradish and sour cream; mix well and season with salt and pepper.

Using about 3 tablespoons per cake, form the potato mixture into 16 discs approximately ½ inch thick. Place the formed cakes in a single layer on sheet pans, cover with plastic wrap or foil, and refrigerate for at least 1½ hours or up to 1 day.

Before cooking coat each cake with the beaten eggs, taking care to completely cover the entire surface of each. Dredge the cakes in the bread crumbs, coating all sides evenly. Return to the refrigerator for 30 minutes, uncovered, or up to 2 hours, covered.

In a very large, nonstick sauté pan, heat about ½ inch of oil over moderately high heat until it is hot, but not smoking. Add some of the cakes, leaving about a ½-inch space between each one.

Cook the first side 2 to 3 minutes, or until golden brown. Flip and cook second side until golden brown. Remove using a slotted spatula and place on paper towels to drain. Keep warm in a low oven. Cook the remaining potato cakes, using more oil for cooking as needed. Serve immediately, drizzled with sour cream.

iced cucumber-horseradish soup

3 large cucumbers, peeled and coarsely chopped

1 small bunch scallions, trimmed and coarsely chopped

4-inch piece fresh horseradish root, peeled and finely chopped

4 cups plain low-fat yogurt

Salt and pepper, to taste

¹/₄ cup minced fresh chives and/or finely chopped mint, for garnish

Cracked ice, optional

➤ At once frigid and fiery, this soup is for hard-core horseradish fiends—and only those who enjoy large intercranial explosions!

HOTTEST 10

makes about 6 servings

In a large bowl, combine the cucumber, scallions, horseradish, and yogurt; mix well. Using a blender, purée in batches until very smooth. Season with salt and pepper. Transfer to a nonreactive container, cover tightly, and refrigerate for at least 6 hours or up to 24 hours.

To serve, ladle into chilled cups or shallow bowls and garnish with chives and/or fresh mint. You may add a couple of tablespoons of finely cracked ice to each bowl to add to the visual effect and to further reduce the temperature of the soup.

tomato and cucumber aspic with horseradish

Place the water in a large bowl. Sprinkle the gelatin over the surface and let stand, undisturbed, 5 to 7 minutes at room temperature.

In a medium saucepan, heat the tomato juice, shallots, and honey over moderate heat until the mixture just begins to boil. Add 1 cup of the tomato juice to the gelatin mixture, stirring constantly to dissolve the gelatin. Slowly add the remaining tomato juice, stirring constantly. Cool to room temperature. When cool, add the horseradish and bell pepper; mix well. Season with salt and pepper. Pour into mold(s) and refrigerate 4 to 6 hours, or until completely set.

To unmold: Set the gelatin molds in a pan filled with hot water for 30 seconds, or until the sides just begin to soften. Remove the pan from the water. Place a flat plate or platter firmly over the surface of the molds and, using one swift movement, flip the two over together, so the aspic is transferred onto the plate. Serve immediately.

➤ Serve this powerful jelled "Bloody Mary" for brunch or lunch with a tossed green salad or German-style potato salad.

Make the aspic in attractive, individual gelatin molds or in one four-cup mold, or double the recipe and use a large eight-cup mold. Individual one-cup capacity angel food cake pans make a particularly handsome presentation—even more dramatic when the center contains a shot of iced vodka!

HOTTEST 7

makes 4 servings

¹/₃ cup cold water

2 envelopes unflavored gelatin

2¹/₂ cups tomato juice

2 shallots, trimmed and thinly sliced

1¹/₂ tablespoons honey

¹/₃ cup prepared horseradish

1 medium green bell pepper, cut into small triangles

Salt and pepper, to taste

horseradish-sesame rice balls with cucumber

3 cups homemade vegetable stock (page 13) or canned vegetable broth (preferably low-sodium)

1 1/2 tablespoons unsalted butter

1 cup medium-grain pearl rice

1/3 cup teriyaki sauce

1 1/2 tablespoons prepared cream-style horseradish

Salt and pepper, to taste

1 small cucumber, peeled, halved, seeded, and cut into 1/2-inch dice

1 to 1 1/2 cups sesame seeds, for coating balls

➤ Garnished with bell peppers cut into fanciful shapes, these feisty cucumber-filled rice balls make a terrific hors d'oeuvre for a formal cocktail party. Drizzled with sour cream or served on a bed of lightly dressed Asian greens, they make an outstanding first course.

If you'd like to double-up on the horseradish for additional firepower, substitute a diced chunk of fresh horseradish root for the cucumber, or use both, cutting each of them smaller to accommodate the size of the rice ball.

HOTTEST 7
makes 12 balls; 4 to 6 servings

In a medium saucepan, bring the vegetable stock and butter to boil over high heat. Add the rice and return to the boil, stirring frequently. Reduce the heat to moderately low, cover, and cook 15 minutes. Remove cover and cook an additional 7 or 8 minutes, or until all the liquid has been absorbed and the rice is very tender. Cool to room temperature.

To the rice add the teriyaki sauce and horseradish. Season with salt and pepper and mix well.

Form the mixture into a 15-inch-long cylinder. Cut into twelve equal pieces and form each into a ball. Use your finger to press a cucumber dice into the center of each ball; close over the hole with the rice, forming a smooth ball. Roll each ball in the sesame seeds, taking care to evenly coat all sides. Cover tightly and refrigerate for at least 1 hour and up to 3 hours. Serve slightly chilled.

Green Bean Salad with Creamy Almond-Horseradish Dressing

THE COMBINATION OF TOASTED ALMONDS AND FRESH HORSERADISH MAKES A SURPRISINGLY BALANCED AND
TASTY DRESSING FOR FRESH GREEN BEANS AND SWEET, CRISP RED BELL PEPPER. PAIR WITH COOKED AND COOLED SLICED HAM,
TURKEY, OR PORK LOIN FOR A WARM-WEATHER LUNCH OR SUPPER.

MAKES ABOUT 6 SERVINGS. ∾ HOT #3

CREAMY ALMOND-HORSERADISH DRESSING:

1 cup walnut or cold-pressed peanut oil

⅓ cup white wine vinegar or champagne vinegar

4-inch piece fresh horseradish root, peeled and coarsely chopped

⅔ cup finely chopped toasted almonds

2 shallots, halved and thinly sliced

½ cup finely chopped fresh parsley

2 pounds green beans, trimmed

1 medium red bell pepper, stemmed, seeded, and cut into slivers

Salt and pepper, to taste

½ cup coarsely chopped toasted almonds, for garnish

TO MAKE THE CREAMY ALMOND-HORSERADISH DRESSING: Place the oil, vinegar, horseradish, and finely chopped almonds in a blender. Puree until smooth, stopping occasionally to scrape the sides of the container. Transfer the dressing to a large bowl; add the shallots and parsley and mix well.

Bring 5 quarts of salted water to boil in an 8-quart pot. Have ready a very large bowl filled with ice water. Add the green beans to the boiling water, stir well, and return to the boil. Cook 1 to 2 minutes, or until they are bright green and crisp-tender. Drain immediately in a colander and refresh with cold running water. Immediately plunge the beans into the ice water and swish them around with your hands. When the beans are thoroughly chilled, about 5 minutes, drain in a colander. Dry the green beans in a single layer on kitchen towels or on several layers of paper towels.

Add the green beans to the dressing along with the red bell pepper; toss gently and season with salt and pepper. Serve immediately, garnished with the coarsely chopped almonds.

horseradish cream cheese–stuffed cucumbers

2 large cucumbers, peeled

8 ounces natural cream cheese, softened to room temperature

4-inch piece fresh horseradish root, peeled and minced

Salt and pepper, to taste

1 bunch fresh chives, halved, for garnish

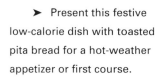

➤ Present this festive low-calorie dish with toasted pita bread for a hot-weather appetizer or first course.

HOTTER 6

makes about 5 servings

Place the cucumber on a cutting board. Position the knife on one tip of the cucumber at a 45-degree angle and cut through. Move the knife about 1½ inches down and make a cut straight across the cucumber, so that you have a 1½-inch-long section of cucumber with one straight end and one angled end. Continue cutting both cucumbers in this fashion, alternating the 45-degree angle cut and the straight-across cut. You should have approximately ten sections from the two cucumbers.

Using a small spoon, starting from the angled end remove the seeds and pulp from the center of each section, leaving a thin layer of flesh on the bottom of the straight end to prevent the filling from falling out the bottom. Gently dry the insides of each piece with a paper towel.

In a small bowl using an electric mixer, beat the cream cheese and horseradish until thoroughly combined, soft, and fluffy. Season with salt and pepper.

Fill each cucumber section with the cream cheese–horseradish mixture, dividing equally. Make small bundles using three or four chives per cucumber section, and anchor the cut ends of the bundle straight up into the cream cheese in each. Serve immediately.

New Potato Salad with Sour Cream—Horseradish Dressing

BECAUSE THIS ROBUST POTATO SALAD HAS THE SINUS-CLEARING QUALITIES ASSOCIATED WITH FRESH HORSERADISH, IT HOLDS UP WELL TO GRILLED OR ROASTED MEATS, WILD POULTRY, OR STRONG-TASTING, OILY FISH. WHEN PAIRED WITH SLICED HAM, SMOKED TURKEY, OR ROAST BEEF, IT FORMS A SIMPLE, HOT-WEATHER MEAL. THIS DISH IS BEST MADE ONE DAY AHEAD.

MAKES ABOUT 6 SERVINGS. ∾ HOTTER #4

2½ pounds small red new potatoes, quartered

1 small red onion, cut into small dice

2 cups sour cream

⅓ cup apple cider vinegar

4-inch piece fresh horseradish root, peeled and finely grated

½ cup finely chopped fresh parsley

Salt and pepper, to taste

In a 10-gallon pot, bring 6 gallons of salted water to a boil. Add the potatoes and return to the boil. Reduce the heat to moderately high, and cook 12 or 13 minutes, or until tender when pierced with a fork. Drain well in a colander and cool to room temperature. When cool, place in a large bowl.

Combine the red onion, sour cream, vinegar, horseradish, and parsley in a small bowl; mix well. Add to the potatoes and mix gently. Season with salt and pepper and serve immediately, or store in a tightly sealed container in the refrigerator for up to 4 days.

poached tofu and green beans with wasabi glaze

To make the wasabi glaze, in a small bowl, combine the wasabi powder and vinegar; mix well to form a smooth paste. Add the peanut oil, teriyaki sauce, and sesame oil; mix well and set aside.

Place the block of tofu on a flat surface. Cut in half lengthwise. Cut each half into 4 equal sections. Using 3 green beans per tofu square, carefully insert the beans through the center and out the other side of each square, so that the tips are exposed on either side.

In a large skillet, bring the vegetable stock to boil over moderate heat. Add the tofu squares, cover, and cook 2 to 3 minutes per side, or until the tofu is slightly tender to the touch. Remove with a slotted spatula and drain on paper towels. The tofu either can be served immediately or covered and refrigerated until chilled, up to 3 hours. Drizzle with the glaze and garnish with the sesame seeds before serving.

➤ Firm tofu and green beans form a striking visual presentation in this low-fat, Japanese-inspired dish. It makes a stunning first course or, paired with ginger-accented buckwheat noodles or miso-laced rice, a healthful and elegant main course.

HOT 2

makes about 4 servings

WASABI GLAZE:

¼ cup wasabi powder

2 tablespoons seasoned rice wine vinegar

2 tablespoons peanut oil

1 tablespoon teriyaki sauce

½ teaspoon Asian sesame oil

14 ounces firm tofu (1 block)

24 small thin green beans (about ½ pound), blanched

2 cups homemade vegetable stock (page 13) or canned vegetable broth (preferably low-sodium)

Black sesame seeds, for garnish

Twice-Baked Potatoes with Horseradish Cream

Rich, filling, and satisfying, these baked potatoes with a cheesy horseradish filling are great with grilled meats or chicken, or served with sausages for a hearty breakfast.
Makes 5 or 10 servings.   Hotter: rated 6

Preheat oven to 400° F.

Bake the potatoes on the middle rack of the oven until tender when pierced with a fork, about 1 hour and 10 minutes. Remove from the oven and slice in half, lengthwise. Using a spoon, carefully scoop out the potato pulp, taking care not to break the skin. Place pulp in a bowl.

Meanwhile, cook the bacon until crisp. Remove with a slotted spoon and drain on paper towels. Finely chop and add to the potato pulp. Cook the diced onion and spices in the remaining bacon fat over moderately high heat for 10 minutes, stirring frequently. Add the green onions and cook for 1 minute. Remove with a slotted spoon and add to the potato-bacon mixture along with the cheddar cheese, sour cream, and horseradish. Mix well and season with salt and pepper.

Divide the mixture among the potato shells, mounding the filling. Bake filled potatoes in a lightly greased baking pan for 25 to 30 minutes, or until the filling is hot. Garnish with minced parsley and serve immediately.

5 very large baking potatoes, scrubbed clean

1 pound sliced bacon

1 large onion, cut in small dice

1 teaspoon fennel seed

½ teaspoon celery seed

1 bunch green onions, trimmed and finely chopped

½ pound sharp cheddar cheese, grated

1 cup sour cream

6-inch piece horseradish root, peeled and grated

Salt and pepper, to taste

½ cup minced parsley, for garnish

potato-horseradish croquettes

Preheat oven to 400° F.

Bake the potatoes in the center of the oven 50 to 55 minutes, or until very tender when pierced with a fork. Remove from the oven and cool to room temperature. Halve potatoes lengthwise and, using a fork, gently scrape pulp into a large bowl. Add the scallions, horseradish, and whole egg and stir well with a fork (to prevent the mixture from becoming gummy). Season well with salt and pepper. Cover and refrigerate for at least 2 hours or up to 8 hours.

To shape the croquettes, using about 2 rounded tablespoons per croquette, form the chilled potato mixture into small balls. Place the beaten eggs in a shallow bowl, and the bread crumbs in a pie plate or shallow baking dish. Dip each croquette into the beaten eggs, taking care to completely cover. Gently roll in the bread crumbs, again taking care to completely cover each croquette. Set aside on a pan lightly dusted with bread crumbs. (Although the croquettes are best cooked right away, if you are pressed for time, you may cover them loosely and refrigerate for up to 3 hours before cooking.)

In a large, shallow-sided pot, heat 2 cups of the oil over moderately high heat until very hot, but not smoking. Add the croquettes in batches (do not crowd or they will not cook properly), and fry, turning as they brown, until toasty brown on all sides. Remove with a slotted spoon and drain on paper towels. Cook the remaining croquettes in this fashion, adding more oil to the pot as needed, and letting it heat to the correct temperature before adding more croquettes. After draining on paper towels, the cooked croquettes may be kept warm on a baking sheet in a 250° F. oven for 7 or 8 minutes before serving. Serve warm, garnished with sprigs of chives or fresh herbs.

➤ These little savory nuggets are irresistible, especially when served with ice-cold ale. Accompany the croquettes with sautéed mixed vegetables or a cold vegetable platter for a full meal.

HOT 3

makes 22 croquettes; 6 to 8 servings

2 large baking potatoes (about 1 3/4 pounds)

4 scallions, trimmed and finely chopped

5-inch piece fresh horseradish, peeled and minced

1 whole egg, plus 2 eggs, lightly beaten

Salt and pepper, to taste

1 1/2 cups finely ground dried bread crumbs

2 1/2 to 3 cups vegetable oil, for frying

Fresh chives or herb sprigs, for garnish

Roast Beef and Vegetable Rolls with Horseradish Cream Cheese

THESE PALATE-TINGLING ROAST BEEF AND VEGETABLE ROLLS MAKE A HANDSOME APPETIZER IDEAL
FOR SERVING AT COCKTAIL PARTIES. THEY ARE SIMPLE TO ASSEMBLE, REQUIRE NO LAST MINUTE PREPARATION,
AND ARE SURE TO PLEASE MEAT- AND VEGETABLE-LOVERS ALIKE.

MAKES ABOUT 8 SERVINGS. ⁓ **HOTTER #5**

TO MAKE THE HORSERADISH CREAM CHEESE: In a medium bowl, combine the cream cheese, horseradish, and lemon zest and mix well.

In a 6-quart pot, bring 4 quarts of salted water to boil over high heat. Have ready a large bowl filled with ice water. Add the green beans and carrots to the boiling water, stir well, and return to the boil. Cook approximately 30 seconds or until both are crisp-tender. Drain well in a colander and refresh with cold running water. Immediately submerge in the ice water, swishing the vegetables around with your hands. When the vegetables are thoroughly chilled, about 5 minutes, drain in a colander. Dry the vegetables in a single layer on kitchen towels or on several layers of paper towels.

Lay the slices of roast beef on a flat surface. Using a wide, dull knife, gently spread about 1½ tablespoons of the cream cheese mixture on each slice. For each roll, make a stack using two green beans, two carrot sticks, and two strips of the bell pepper on top of the cream cheese along the short end of each beef slice. Gently roll the beef around the vegetables, forming a tight cylinder (the tips of the green beans will probably peek out the end of each roll).

Wrap the finished rolls in plastic and refrigerate for at least 1 hour or up to 4 hours. Just before serving, cut each roll in half to expose the cross-section. Serve immediately.

HORSERADISH CREAM CHEESE:

1 pound natural cream cheese (no gums or stabilizers), softened to room temperature

5-inch piece fresh horseradish root, peeled and finely grated

Zest from 1 lemon

⅓ to ½ pound (about 24) green beans, trimmed

2 carrots, cut into 24 sticks approximately 3 inches long and ¼ inch wide

Twelve ⅛-inch-thick slices rare roast beef (about 1 pound)

1 large yellow bell pepper, stemmed, seeded, and cut into 24 long, thin strips

Smoked Ham and Cabbage Slaw with Horseradish

DELICIOUS ON ITS OWN, YOU MAY ALSO WANT TO TEAM THIS ZESTY COLESLAW WITH
FRIED FISH OR GRILLED CHICKEN FOR A COMPLETE MEAL.
MAKES ABOUT 6 SERVINGS. HOTTER #4

Place the cabbage, red onion, and ham in a very large bowl. Place the olive oil in a small bowl. Slowly add the vinegar, whisking constantly with a wire whisk to form a smooth emulsion. Add the prepared horseradish, fresh horseradish, cumin seeds, and sugar; mix well. Add to the cabbage-ham mixture and toss gently. Season with salt and pepper. Serve immediately, or store in a tightly sealed container in the refrigerator for up to 3 days (bearing in mind that the vinegar will cause the cabbage to wilt slightly).

5 cups white cabbage, finely shredded

1 small red onion, halved and thinly sliced

*¾ pound thinly sliced smoked ham,
    cut into ¼-inch-wide strips*

½ cup olive oil

¼ cup apple cider vinegar

½ cup prepared horseradish

*5-inch piece fresh horseradish root, peeled and
    finely grated*

1½ teaspoons cumin seeds

1 teaspoon sugar

Salt and pepper, to taste

fried egg and potato hash with horseradish

4 medium red or white
potatoes (about 2 pounds),
cut into ½-inch dice

3 tablespoons peanut or
vegetable oil

4-inch piece fresh
horseradish, peeled and
finely chopped

1 green bell pepper, cut
into small dice

3 tablespoons prepared
cream-style horseradish

8 eggs

➤ This palate-stimulating
breakfast or brunch dish will
send a wake-up call to even the
most tired taste buds. To complete the meal, serve with
buttered rye toast and glasses
of tomato juice.

HOT 3
makes 4 servings

In a very large, nonstick sauté pan, cook the potatoes in 2 tablespoons of the oil over moderately high heat 10 to 12 minutes until golden brown, stirring frequently. Add the fresh horseradish and bell pepper and cook 2 minutes, stirring constantly. Add the prepared horseradish and mix well. Transfer to an ovenproof dish and keep warm in a 250° F. oven.

Taking care to leave the yolks intact, crack the eggs into a large bowl. Heat the remaining tablespoon of oil in the sauté pan over moderate heat. When the oil is hot but not smoking, pour in all of the eggs, again taking care to keep yolks intact as you add them to the pan. Cook the eggs until set on underside, then gently flip to cook second side (it's okay if a few yolks break). Alternatively, you may cover the eggs and cook without flipping over moderately low heat until set. (Using this method they won't have as much "fried egg" taste, texture, or appearance; it's a matter of your preference.)

Add the eggs to the potato-horseradish mixture and mix gently (the yolks will break and create a delicious golden "sauce"). Serve immediately.

Smoked Chicken Salad with Horseradish Vinaigrette

LESS PUNGENT WHEN FINELY DICED RATHER THAN GRATED, THE HORSERADISH IN THIS DISH ADDS FLAVOR WITH
LESS HEAT, MAKING IT SUITABLE FOR THOSE WITH MORE SENSITIVE PALATES. IF YOU CANNOT FIND WHOLE SMOKED CHICKENS,
FEEL FREE TO USE SMOKED CHICKEN BREAST OR SMOKED TURKEY BREAST CUT INTO CUBES.

MAKES ABOUT 4 SERVINGS. ⁓ **HOT #2**

TO MAKE THE HORSERADISH VINAIGRETTE: Place the peanut oil in a large bowl. Slowly add the vinegar, whisking constantly with a wire whisk to form a smooth emulsion. Add the horseradish and caraway seeds and mix well.

Add the chicken and celery to the vinaigrette, season with salt and pepper, and mix well. Arrange the large butter lettuce leaves around the edge of a large platter and put the small leaves in the center. Mound the salad on top of the small lettuce leaves and garnish with the tomatoes. Serve immediately.

HORSERADISH VINAIGRETTE:

⅔ cup peanut oil

3 tablespoons rice wine vinegar or champagne vinegar

3-inch piece fresh horseradish root, peeled and cut into tiny dice

1 teaspoon caraway seeds

2½ cups shredded smoked chicken meat

2 inner stalks celery, trimmed, thinly sliced on the diagonal, and blanched

Salt and pepper, to taste

6 large butter lettuce leaves, trimmed

6 to 8 small inner butter lettuce leaves, trimmed

4 cherry tomatoes, halved, for garnish

4 yellow pear tomatoes, halved, for garnish

Grilled Mackerel with Horseradish

Pleasantly oily mackerel is a natural companion to the piquant flavors of horse-radish. Sauced with only a few assertive ingredients and grilled over hot coals, this dish allows the true flavors of both the fish and the horseradish to come through with clarity and depth.
Makes 4 servings.   *Hotter: rated 4*

Coat the fish with some of the olive oil, and dust with black pepper. Prepare a charcoal grill. When the coals are medium hot (the coals will have a thin layer of gray ash), place the fish on the grill and cook for 7 to 8 minutes. Carefully flip the fish over and cook the second side for 6 to 7 minutes, or until the fish is opaque all the way through. Remove from the grill and arrange on a bed of the parsley on a large platter.

Heat the remaining oil, the horseradish, the red pepper flakes and rosemary, and the lemon juice in a small saucepan over moderate heat. Cook for 1 to 2 minutes, or until the bits of horseradish begin to sizzle. Remove from the heat and drizzle over the fish. Garnish with the rosemary and thyme sprigs and serve immediately.

4 1-pound mackerels, head on and cleaned

¾ cup olive oil

Black pepper

2 cups parsley sprigs

4-inch piece fresh horseradish root, peeled and finely chopped

1 teaspoon each dried red pepper flakes and rosemary

⅓ cup fresh lemon juice

Rosemary and thyme sprigs, for garnish

German Horseradish Sauce

This German sauce is quite mild. It is very good with wild game and poultry, though it is traditionally served with boiled meats or sausage. For a more assertive flavor, add an extra ¼ cup of uncooked, grated horseradish just before serving.
Makes about 1¼ cups.   *Hot: rated 2*

Place 1 cup of the horseradish and the thyme and butter in a saucepan. Cook over moderate heat for 2 to 3 minutes, stirring all the while. Add the beef broth and bread crumbs and bring to a boil over high heat, stirring constantly. Reduce the heat to moderate and cook for 10 minutes. Add the sherry and remaining horseradish and cook 2 minutes. Season with salt and pepper and serve warm.

5- to 6-inch piece horseradish root, peeled and grated

½ teaspoon dried thyme

4 tablespoons (½ stick) unsalted butter

1¼ cups unsalted beef broth or stock

¼ cup fine dry bread crumbs

⅓ cup dry sherry

Salt and pepper, to taste

Horseradish-Crusted Salmon

2 eggs, lightly beaten

½ cup whole milk

8-inch piece horseradish root, peeled and grated

1 teaspoon salt

4   8-ounce salmon fillets

¼ cup light olive oil

The first time I had horseradish paired with salmon I thought it would overwhelm the delicate, sweet flavor of the fish, but the combination was really exciting and quite successful. The crust adds flavor and helps to seal in the juices of the fish. A drizzle of crème fraîche or thinned sour cream is a pleasing garnish for this savory fish fillet.

Makes 4 servings.   *Hot: rated 2*

In a shallow baking dish large enough to accommodate all the fillets, combine the eggs, milk, horseradish root, and salt; mix well. Pat the salmon dry with paper towels. Coat each piece of salmon with the horseradish batter, taking care to press the horseradish onto all sides of the fish.

Heat the olive oil in a nonstick sauté pan large enough to accommodate all the fish. When the oil is hot, but not smoking, add the fish and cook over moderately high heat for 3 to 4 minutes on the first side. Carefully flip the fish over and cook the second side for 3 to 4 minutes. Do not overcook the fish or it will be dry and tasteless. Remove from the pan and serve immediately.

Pan-Fried Trout on Spinach with Bacon and Horseradish

PAN-FRIED TROUT IS ONE OF MY FAVORITE BREAKFAST DISHES. IN THIS RECIPE, THE DELICATE FLAVOR OF THE FISH IS ACCENTED BY SMOKY BACON, PUNGENT HORSERADISH, AND FRESH SPINACH, RESULTING IN A MEDLEY OF CONTRASTING FLAVORS, TEXTURES, AND COLORS.

To facilitate chopping the bacon, wrap it tightly in plastic and place in the freezer for twenty minutes prior to cutting.

MAKES 4 SERVINGS. ∾ **HOT #1**

¾ pound thick-sliced bacon, coarsely chopped

4 boneless trout filets (6 to 8 ounces each)

All-purpose flour, for dredging

2½ tablespoons peanut oil

Juice from 1 lemon

3-inch piece fresh horseradish root, peeled and minced

1 large bunch spinach, stemmed, washed, and dried (about 4 cups packed leaves)

Salt and pepper, to taste

Lemon wedges, for garnish

In a large nonstick sauté pan, cook the bacon until brown and crisp. Remove with a slotted spoon and drain on paper towels; set aside. Remove the bacon fat from the pan, reserving 2 tablespoons for cooking and discarding the rest. Wipe the sauté pan clean of any remaining brown bits and return the reserved bacon fat to the pan. Set aside until needed.

Using a clean kitchen towel, pat the trout filets dry on both sides. Dredge the fish in flour, taking care to coat all sides. In a very large sauté pan, heat the peanut oil over moderately high heat until hot, but not smoking. Add the trout, skin sides down, and cook 2 minutes, or until light golden brown. Flip the fish over, add the lemon juice, and reduce the heat to moderate. Cook the second sides 3 to 4 minutes, or until the fish is barely opaque in the center. Remove from the pan, cover with foil, and set aside.

Heat the reserved bacon fat over moderate heat. Add the horseradish, spinach, and reserved bacon and cook, stirring constantly, 30 to 45 seconds, or until the spinach just starts to wilt. Immediately remove from the heat and season with salt and pepper. Arrange the spinach mixture on 1 large platter or divide among 4 individual plates. Place the trout on top of the spinach and serve immediately, garnished with lemon wedges.

Lamb and Horseradish Tartlettes

The savory filling for these individual tartlettes is best if made 1 or 2 days in advance. The dough can also be made a couple of days ahead, so this would be an ideal appetizer or light lunch for company. A salad of sweet and bitter greens or a green bean salad would go nicely with these little pies. Serve with prepared horseradish if you prefer a more pronounced flavor.
Makes 6 4-inch tartlettes.   *Hot: rated 1*

To make the dough: Place the flour and salt in a medium-sized bowl; mix well. Add the shortening and butter and, using your hands, mix lightly and quickly until the mixture resembles coarse meal. Add enough water to make the dough come together and form a ball. Wrap in plastic and refrigerate for 2 hours or up to 2 days.

Preheat oven to 350° F.

Divide the dough into 6 balls. Lightly dust a flat surface with flour. Using a rolling pin, roll each ball into a 5-inch circle. Gently press each circle into a tart pan, making the sides extend a bit higher than the pan. (The dough shrinks a bit during baking; this way the crust will be high enough to hold all the filling.) Prick the bottom of the dough with a fork, and bake for 10 minutes.

To make the filling: In a large sauté pan, cook the onion and garlic in the olive oil over moderate heat for 10 minutes, stirring frequently. Add the lamb, coriander, and fennel seed, and cook for 5 minutes, or until the meat loses its pink color. Add the tomatoes and sherry and bring to a boil over high heat. Reduce the heat to moderate and cook for 35 to 40 minutes, or until the liquids have evaporated, the meat is tender, and the mixture is fairly thick. Add the parsley and horseradish and cook for 2 to 3 minutes, stirring all the while. Remove from the heat and cool slightly. Add the cheese; mix well, and season with salt and pepper.

Fill each shell with the filling. Bake at 350° F. for 30 to 35 minutes or until the filling is hot and browned. Remove from the oven and serve immediately.

Dough:

1½ cups all-purpose flour

¼ teaspoon salt

4 tablespoons chilled vegetable shortening

4 tablespoons (½ stick) unsalted butter, cut into 6 pieces

2 to 3 tablespoons ice water

Filling:

1 large onion, cut in small dice

3 cloves garlic, minced

3 tablespoons olive oil

1 pound lamb stew meat, finely chopped (not minced or ground)

1 teaspoon each ground coriander and fennel seed

1½ cups chopped tomatoes

¾ cup dry sherry

1 cup chopped parsley

6-inch piece horseradish root, peeled and grated

½ pound feta cheese, crumbled

Salt and pepper, to taste

Horseradish-Stuffed Pork Loin

This stuffed pork loin makes an outstanding presentation. Have your butcher cut a "pocket" in the pork loin for the colorful stuffing. The recipe makes enough stuffing for two pork loins, or enough to fill one and to bake a separate dish of stuffing. With roasted new potatoes or rice, or the extra stuffing, and a green vegetable, this dish is good to serve for company, since it is easy and fast. Offer prepared horseradish alongside the roast if you yearn for more horseradish flavor. Makes 4 to 6 servings. *Hot: rated 1*

½ pound thick sliced bacon

1 large onion, cut in small dice

3 cloves garlic, minced

4 tablespoons (½ stick) unsalted butter

2 teaspoons each dried thyme, sage, and basil

1 large green apple, cored, and cut in small dice

4-inch piece horseradish root, peeled and minced

¾ cup dried cranberries or dried pitted cherries

1 cup Madeira

2 cups dried cornbread crumbs

Salt and pepper, to taste

1 2½-pound boned pork loin, with a pocket cut for stuffing

1 cup prepared horseradish (optional)

Sage sprigs, for garnish

Preheat oven to 450° F.

In a large sauté pan, cook the bacon until it is crisp, remove with a slotted spoon, and drain on paper towels. Chop coarsely and place in a large bowl. Discard all but 3 tablespoons of the fat, and transfer this to a large, deep-sided skillet.

Cook the onion and garlic in the bacon fat over moderate heat for 15 minutes, stirring from time to time. Add the butter, spices, apple, horseradish, and cranberries and cook over moderate heat for 5 minutes. Add the Madeira and the cornbread crumbs and cook over high heat for 3 to 4 minutes, stirring all the while to mix the ingredients thoroughly. Remove from the heat, add to the bacon, mix well, and season with salt and pepper.

Place half of the stuffing in a small baking dish and cover with foil. Gently stuff the remainder into the pocket of the loin, pressing the stuffing all the way into the pocket and making the loin round with stuffing. Tie with kitchen string to secure the opening and keep the shape of the meat.

Fill a shallow baking pan with water to a depth of 2 inches. Place the pork loin on a flat roasting rack set inside the pan. Roast for 30 minutes at 450° F. Reduce the heat to 400° F. and roast for 20 to 25 minutes more, or until the meat has lost its pink color and the stuffing is hot. Do not overcook the meat or it will be tough, dry, and tasteless.

Let the pork stand at room temperature for 8 to 10 minutes before cutting. Slice into 1-inch rounds, garnish with sage sprigs, and serve immediately, with additional prepared horseradish if desired.

Three-Sausage Stew with Horseradish and Greens

2 large onions, cut in medium wedges

4 cloves garlic, thinly sliced

¼ cup olive oil

1 rounded teaspoon each dried thyme, oregano, basil, and rosemary

2 cups dry white wine

2 cups chopped and seeded tomatoes

6-inch piece fresh horseradish root, peeled and finely chopped

½ pound hot Polish sausage, cut in ½-inch rounds

1 pound sweet Italian sausage, cut in ½-inch rounds

1 pound garlic sausage, cut in ½-inch rounds

1 large bunch Swiss chard, stemmed and very coarsely chopped

Salt and pepper, to taste

Fresh herb sprigs, for garnish

Fresh horseradish root adds texture to this hearty meat-lover's stew, while complementing flavorful sausages. The horseradish loses much of its pungency through cooking, adding just the right zing to this cold-weather dish. Serve with country-style bread, baked potatoes or noodles, and dark beer.
Makes 4 to 6 servings.   Hotter: rated 6

In a large deep-sided pan, cook the onions and garlic in the olive oil over moderate heat for 15 to 20 minutes, stirring frequently. Add the herbs and 1 cup of the wine and cook for 10 minutes over high heat. Add tomatoes, horseradish, sausages, and remaining wine and cook for 5 minutes over high heat.

Reduce the heat to moderate and cook for 15 minutes, or until the sausages are tender and cooked. Do not overcook the sausages or they will be dry and tough. Add the Swiss chard just before serving, or ladle the stew onto a bed of the greens. Season with salt and pepper, and garnish with fresh herb sprigs.

Beef and Watercress Sandwiches
with Horseradish Cream Cheese

I remember my Mom telling me about the watercress sandwiches she had at a bridge party 50 years ago—watercress, butter, and white bread. That isn't my idea of great food, much less lunch, but I think these sandwiches could qualify as a real meal. If you are pressed for time you can buy sliced roast beef, making just the cream cheese at home.
Makes about 6 servings.   *Hotter: rated 4*

Heat the olive oil in a sauté pan large enough to accommodate the steaks. When the oil is hot, add the meat and cook over moderately high heat for 2 to 3 minutes per side, or until the meat is medium rare and the outside is browned. Remove from the pan and let stand at room temperature for 10 minutes before slicing. Slice into thin pieces and set aside until needed.

Meanwhile, combine the cream cheese, horseradish, minced chives, and black pepper in a small bowl. Spread each slice of bread with some of the cream cheese mixture. Top half the slices with a few sprigs of watercress. Arrange some slices of beef on top of the watercress, and cover with a few more sprigs of watercress and the second slice of bread. Press gently to secure the ingredients and garnish with the whole chives and yellow cherry tomatoes. Serve at room temperature.

2 tablespoons olive oil

1½ pounds filet mignon, trimmed of excess fat

1 pound natural cream cheese (no gums or preservatives)

5- to 6-inch piece horseradish root, peeled and grated

⅓ cup minced chives

Black pepper, to taste

1 large bunch watercress, stemmed

12 slices firm whole wheat or country-style bread

Whole chives, for garnish

Yellow cherry tomatoes, for garnish

Pork Tenderloin and Cucumber Sandwiches with Horseradish Mayonnaise

PAIR THIS HEARTY SANDWICH WITH A MUG OF DARK BEER AND THICK-CUT POTATO CHIPS FOR A SATISFYING AUTUMN LUNCH. THE COMPONENTS FOR THIS RECIPE CAN ALL BE PREPARED ONE DAY IN ADVANCE AND ASSEMBLED JUST BEFORE SERVING. MAKES 4 SANDWICHES. ～ HOTTER #6

HORSERADISH MAYONNAISE:

2 egg yolks, vigorously beaten

1 whole egg, vigorously beaten

½ cup peanut or vegetable oil

¼ cup olive oil

2 teaspoons sherry vinegar

5-inch piece fresh horseradish root, peeled and finely grated

Salt and pepper, to taste

Two ⅔- to ¾-pound pork tenderloins, trimmed of fat

4 tablespoons prepared horseradish

8 thick slices oversized dark bread, such as whole-wheat, nine-grain, or pumpernickel

1 English cucumber, peeled and thinly sliced

TO MAKE THE HORSERADISH MAYONNAISE: Place the egg yolks and whole egg in a medium bowl. Using an electric hand-mixer on low speed, begin adding the peanut oil to the eggs, one drop at a time, beating constantly to form a smooth emulsion. When all the peanut oil has been added, add the olive oil in a very thin stream, beating constantly to maintain a smooth emulsion. Add the vinegar and horseradish and mix well. Season with salt and pepper. Store in a tightly sealed container in the refrigerator until ready to use.

Preheat oven to 450° F.

Coat the pork tenderloins on all sides with the prepared horseradish. Place the tenderloins on a flat, greased roasting rack set over a lightly greased baking dish. Roast for 10 to 12 minutes, or until the center is just barely pink. Take care not to overcook the pork. Remove from the oven and cool to room temperature. When cool, cut into thin slices. (If time allows, wrap the cooked and cooled tenderloins in plastic or foil and refrigerate for 1 day. Thoroughly chilled meat is much easier to cut into thin slices, and the meat keeps well.)

Evenly distribute the Horseradish Mayonnaise among the bread slices, spreading an even layer on each. Arrange 5 or 6 rounds of cucumber on 4 of the bread slices and top with the sliced pork. Cover each with a second slice of bread and press gently to secure the filling. Cut in half and serve immediately.

grilled smoked cheddar cheese sandwiches with horseradish and tomato

2 to 3 tablespoons prepared cream-style horseradish

2 large slices good-quality, firm whole-wheat or rye bread

1/4 pound smoked Cheddar cheese, thinly sliced

3 thin slices tomato

1 tablespoon peanut or vegetable oil (approximately), for cooking

➤ This recipe gives directions for making one large sandwich. It easily can be increased in quantity to fit your needs, which may be greater than initially planned once you taste this flavor-packed lunch treat.

HOTTER 4

makes 1 sandwich; 1 serving

Spread the horseradish on one side of each bread slice. Cover the horseradish on one slice with half of the cheese. Top with the tomatoes and cover with the remaining cheese. Cover with the second slice of bread, horseradish-side down. Press gently to secure the sandwich.

In a small sauté pan, heat half of the oil over moderately low heat until warm. Add the sandwich, cover, and cook on one side until the bread is toasty brown and the cheese begins to melt, 4 or 5 minutes. Using a spatula, carefully flip the sandwich over; add the remaining ½ tablespoon oil (you may need to add more oil if the pan is very dry, and the bread is absorbing a lot of oil). Cook second side 4 or 5 minutes, or until all the cheese has melted and the bread is toasty brown. Remove and drain on paper towels, if necessary. Serve immediately.

Rigatoni with Prawns and Horseradish-Leek Cream

THE PLEASING SHARP TASTE OF FRESH HORSERADISH COUNTERBALANCES THE RICH QUALITY OF HEAVY CREAM
AND FRESH PRAWNS IN THIS SIMPLE-TO-MAKE PASTA DISH. TO ROUND OFF THE MEAL, SERVE WITH A SALAD OF
MILD AND BITTER GREENS AND WARM BREAD.

MAKES ABOUT 6 SERVINGS. ~ **HOT #2**

Wash the sliced leeks in a large bowl of cold water, swishing them about with your hands and loosening any dirt or sand from between the layers. Remove the leeks from the water and drain well in a colander. If they are particularly sandy, repeat the procedure a second time, draining thoroughly.

In a very large, shallow saucepan, cook the leeks and garlic in the olive oil over high heat for 5 minutes, stirring frequently, until the leeks are wilted and any moisture has evaporated. Add the cream, tomatoes, horseradish, and thyme and bring to a boil over high heat, stirring constantly to prevent the cream from boiling over. Reduce the heat to moderately high and cook 6 to 8 minutes, stirring frequently, until the cream is thick enough to heavily coat the back of a spoon. Add the prawns and cook 30 seconds, or until they are opaque halfway through. Remove from the heat and set aside until needed.

Bring 6 quarts of salted water to boil in a 9-quart pot. Add the pasta and cook 11 to 12 minutes, or until al dente. Drain well in a colander and place in a very large, preheated bowl.

Heat the sauce over high heat for 30 seconds or just until the prawns are opaque in the center. Take care not to overcook the prawns. Add to the pasta, toss gently, and season with salt and pepper. Garnish with the parsley and serve immediately.

2 leeks, white part only, halved, and thinly sliced

2 cloves garlic, finely chopped

2 tablespoons olive oil

2½ cups heavy cream

2 small tomatoes, cored and cut into small dice

4-inch piece fresh horseradish root, peeled and finely grated

1½ teaspoons dried thyme

½ pound medium prawns, peeled

¾ pound rigatoni pasta

Salt and pepper, to taste

½ cup coarsely chopped fresh parsley

rye bread stuffing with toasted almonds and horseradish

In a very large sauté pan, cook the onion and spices in the butter and olive oil over moderate heat 10 minutes, stirring frequently. Add the fresh horseradish and cook 5 minutes, stirring occasionally. Add the bread and increase heat to high. Cook, stirring constantly, 2 to 3 minutes or until bread begins to brown. Add the vegetable stock and cook 3 to 5 minutes, stirring occasionally, until about 2 tablespoons of liquid remain.

Remove from the heat, stir in the prepared horseradish and the almonds, and season with salt and pepper.

May be served immediately or, if you prefer the top browned, transfer to an ovenproof dish, dot with butter, and bake on the upper shelf of a 400° F. oven until golden brown, about 12 minutes.

➤ I relish the combined flavors and textures of horseradish, toasted almonds, and caraway seeds in this classic stuffing-with-a-twist.

Use as a filling for winter squash, zucchini, and eggplant, or serve as is with a drizzle of tomato sauce or a dollop of sour cream.

HOT 2

makes 4 to 6 servings

1 large onion, cut into medium dice

2 teaspoons *each* ground fenugreek and fennel seeds

3 tablespoons unsalted butter

1 1/2 tablespoons olive oil

5-inch piece fresh horseradish root, peeled and minced

10 slices stale rye bread (preferably sourdough), cut into 1/2-inch cubes

2 cups homemade vegetable stock (page 13) or canned vegetable broth (preferably low-sodium)

2 tablespoons prepared cream-style horseradish

1 cup toasted almonds, coarsely chopped

Salt and pepper, to taste

Israeli Horseradish and Beet Condiment

THIS STUNNING CONDIMENT GOES WELL WITH GRILLED MEATS AND POULTRY, BUT IT TRULY COMPLEMENTS OILY, PUNGENT FISH SUCH AS HERRING, MACKEREL, OR SARDINES. FOR A MORE BITING, SHARPLY FLAVORED MIXTURE WITH A HOMOGENIZED TEXTURE, COARSELY GRATE THE COOKED BEETS AND THE HORSERADISH ROOT INSTEAD OF CUTTING THEM INTO THIN STRIPS.

MAKES ABOUT 4 CUPS. ∾ **HOTTER #6**

5 medium red beets, trimmed and washed
6-inch piece fresh horseradish root, peeled
4 cups apple cider vinegar
2½ tablespoons each sugar and kosher salt

Bring 4 quarts of water to boil in a large saucepan. Add the beets and return to the boil. Reduce the heat to moderately high and cook about 15 minutes, or until they yield slightly to the touch but retain a firm interior. Drain in a colander and cool to room temperature. When cool enough to handle, peel the beets and cut into ⅛-inch-thick rounds. Using 3 slices per pile, stack the beet rounds and cut into ⅛-inch-wide strips. Place in a very large bowl and set aside.

Using a very sharp knife, cut the horseradish root crosswise into two 3-inch cylinders. Cut the root lengthwise into ⅛-inch-wide slices. Using three slices per pile, stack the horseradish root and cut into ⅛-inch-wide strips.

Add the horseradish, vinegar, sugar, and salt to the beets and mix gently. Transfer to a glass or stainless steel container with a tight-fitting lid and refrigerate for at least 1 week, preferably 2 weeks, before using. Will keep in the refrigerator for 2 to 3 months.

Hangover Bloody Marys

Jalapeño Pepper Vodka:

1 quart vodka

2 fresh jalapeño peppers, halved

1 quart tomato juice

¾ cup prepared horseradish

¼ cup Worcestershire sauce

¼ cup fresh lime juice

3 tablespoons Tabasco sauce

1 tablespoon each ground celery seed and black pepper

1 teaspoon ground cinnamon

Stalks of celery, trimmed

Lime slices

If in fact you are suffering from a hangover, it might be best to have someone else prepare this mix! On the other hand, if you expect a hangover, make the mix the night before—it will taste even better the second day. If you want to use regular vodka for the cocktails, feel free, but this special peppery version is sensational in Bloody Marys (and even better taken straight from a frozen shot glass). A less traditional garnish would be a pickled jalapeño slit to the stem on the rim of each glass.
Mix makes 4 to 6 servings.   *Hottest: rated 7*

To make the Jalapeño Pepper Vodka: Place the two jalapeño peppers in a bottle of vodka for 2 to 4 days, depending on how hot you like your vodka. Remove the peppers and the vodka is ready to drink. (If you leave the peppers in the vodka indefinitely, the vodka will get hotter and hotter.)

Combine the tomato juice, horseradish, Worcestershire sauce, lime juice, Tabasco sauce, and the spices; mix well and adjust seasoning. Pour the mix into glasses filled with ice cubes, leaving enough room for the vodka. Generally, 1 to 1½ ounces of liquor per 6 ounces of mix is used, but in the case of a hangover as little as a drop or as much as 3 ounces of liquor could be in order. Garnish each glass with a sprinkling of pepper and one stalk of celery or a lime slice. Serve immediately if not sooner.

mustard

USTARD

THROUGH THE CENTURIES MUSTARD HAS BEEN USED FOR MEDICINAL AS WELL AS CULINARY purposes. Ancient Greeks used the seeds for their curative properties and for flavoring foods, or, more accurately, for disguising the taste of rancid meats. It was the Romans, however, who combined the seeds with vinegars, honey, spices, and nuts to form the first prepared mustard pastes. The name is thought to come from the Roman mixture of crushed mustard seeds and *must* (unfermented grape juice), which was called *mustum ardens,* or "burning wine."

A member of the *Cruciferae* family, mustard plants are annuals which produce bright yellow flowers and long, narrow, seed-filled pods. Black mustard, native to the Middle East and Asia, has been cultivated in Europe for centuries. Because this particular seed is difficult to harvest, it has not been widely cultivated for mass production. Brown mustard seed, originally from Asia, now grows throughout northern Europe and in parts of England. Less pungent than its black counterpart, this seed is favored by many mustard makers, who use it to produce full-flavored, pungent pastes. Native to the Mediterranean, yellow mustard seeds are now grown in eastern counties of England, and in Canada and the United States. Less pungent than the black or brown seeds and larger than both, yellow seeds are used primarily in English, French, some German, and many American mustards; they are also ground and sold as mustard powder.

When purchasing whole mustard seeds, look for regular, even-colored, hard seeds. Store them in a tightly sealed jar or plastic bag in a cool, dark place for up to one year. Purchase mustard powder in individual sealed tins rather than in bulk, where it tends to lose its strength and intensity. Prepared commercial mustards must be refrigerated once opened; properly stored, mustards are good for four or five months, but those kept longer tend to lose their potency and flavor.

When mustard seeds are crushed and mixed with cold or warm water, the enzyme myrosin mixes with the glucoside contained in the seeds and forms a volatile oil that is a desirable characteristic of mustard. However, myrosin mixed with boiling water produces a bitter, unpleasant flavor, rendering the finished product undesirable. For this reason, use cold water when making homemade mustards. Like horseradish, fresh ginger, and many chili peppers, prepared mustard loses most of its punch when cooked for extended periods of time. For the most pronounced flavor, add slightly crushed seeds or mustard paste at the end of cooking rather than at the beginning. Whole mustards seeds can be added at any time during the cooking process. Prepared mustards act as a natural thickener, and since mustard is so low in calories and fat, it is a sensible and delicious thickening agent for many dishes.

Commercial mustards range from mild and smooth to sharp, biting, and coarse in texture. When cooking, intensely hot, pungent mustards naturally lend more flavor to cooked or heated dishes than do those with less emphatic properties. Although most mustards are exhilarating to the taste buds, there is a wide spectrum of heat intensity. Likewise, depending on the type of mustard used and the way it is used in a dish, some of the following recipes are tame and understated while others pack a punch. For example, the *Chinese-Style Mouth-Fire Dipping Sauce* is tremendously hot and fiery while the *Caramelized Onion–Mustard Tart with Gruyère Cheese* is mellow and subtle.

The flavor of mustard can take center stage, but it also can work nicely in a supporting cast of flavors, lending nuances to dishes without overwhelming them. Mustard plays a dominant role in dishes such as *Grilled Chicken Wings with Two Mustards and Honey* and *Sweet and Spicy Bell Pepper–Mustard Relish,* but it serves more as a background flavor in *Creamy Mustard-Potato-Leek Gratin* and *Baked Macaroni with Mustard and Cheddar Cheese.*

When blended with other ingredients, mustard takes the role of a flavoring agent rather than one that supplies fire. Still, these tiny little seeds and prepared pastes lend a penetrating, distinctive, and welcome accent to a delectable variety of foods and dishes.

Indian Mango Chutney
with Mustard

Mango gives this chutney a wonderful golden color, and the abundance of mustard seeds adds texture, color, and punch. For extra heat add the optional prepared hot mustard, but I suggest you taste the chutney before doing so. Serve with vegetable or meat dishes, as well as poultry, as pictured here.
Makes about 2½ cups.   Hot: rated 3

In a large sauté pan, cook the onion and jalapeño peppers in the oil over moderate heat for 10 minutes, stirring frequently. Add the garlic, spices, and vinegar and cook for 5 minutes, stirring constantly. Add the mango and lime juice; mix well. Reduce the heat to moderate, and cook for 5 minutes or until the fruit is soft and the mixture is aromatic.

Season the chutney with salt and pepper and taste it for heat; add the prepared hot mustard if desired. Cool to room temperature. Unless serving immediately, store in a covered glass or plastic container in the refrigerator. The chutney will keep for up to 1 month.

1 large onion, cut in small dice

2 jalapeño peppers, minced

3 tablespoons vegetable oil or unsalted butter

3 cloves garlic, minced

3 tablespoons yellow mustard seeds

2 teaspoons each ground coriander, turmeric, and whole black mustard seeds

1 teaspoon each ground cardamom, cumin, and cinnamon

⅓ cup white wine or apple cider vinegar

2 cups finely chopped peeled mango (about 2 large mangoes)

¼ cup fresh lime juice

Salt and pepper, to taste

2 tablespoons prepared hot mustard (optional)

Sweet and Spicy Bell Pepper—Mustard Relish

THIS ASSERTIVE-TASTING, COLORFUL RELISH DEPENDS ON HONEY MUSTARD FOR A MILD, SWEET TONE, COLEMAN'S DRY MUSTARD FOR A SHARP EDGE, AND COARSE-GRAINED MUSTARD FOR BODY AND TEXTURE. EXCELLENT PAIRED WITH SAUSAGES OF ALL VARIETIES, THIS RELISH ALSO CAN BE USED AS AN ACCOMPANIMENT TO ROASTED CHICKEN, PORK, BEEF, OR LAMB, OR AS A CONDIMENT WHEN MAKING SANDWICHES.

MAKES 4 TO 6 SERVINGS. ～ **HOT #2**

In a very large, nonstick sauté pan, cook the onion, coriander, and caraway seeds in the olive oil over high heat for 2 to 3 minutes, stirring frequently. Add the bell peppers and cook 4 to 5 minutes, stirring frequently, until they are just wilted. Remove from the heat and place in a large bowl; cool to room temperature.

In a small bowl, combine the honey and coarse-grained mustards, the dry mustard, and the vinegar; mix well. Add to the vegetables and mix gently. Season with salt and pepper. Transfer to a nonreactive container, cover tightly, and refrigerate for at least 1 day before serving. Will keep in the refrigerator for up to 7 days.

1 medium yellow onion, halved and thinly sliced

2 teaspoons ground coriander

½ teaspoon caraway seeds

2 tablespoons olive oil

1 large red bell pepper, stemmed, seeded, and thinly sliced

1 large green bell pepper, stemmed, seeded, and thinly sliced

1 large yellow or gold bell pepper, stemmed, seeded, and thinly sliced

¼ cup honey mustard

¼ cup coarse-grained mustard

1½ tablespoons Coleman's dry mustard

1½ tablespoons white wine vinegar

Salt and pepper, to taste

Chinese-Style Mouth-Fire Dipping Sauce

PRESENT THIS INTENSELY FLAVORED MUSTARD-BASED DIPPING SAUCE TO THOSE WHO ADORE THE HEAD-TINGLING QUALITIES OF MUSTARD POWDER COMBINED WITH RAW GARLIC AND FIERY CHILI PASTE. "ORIENTAL-STYLE" DRY MUSTARD PACKED IN TINS IS AVAILABLE IN ASIAN MARKETS, SPECIALTY FOOD SHOPS, AND MOST GROCERY STORES.

MAKES ABOUT 1 CUP. ∼ **HOTTEST #9**

½ cup "Oriental-Style" dry mustard

¾ cup cold water

2 tablespoons soy sauce

1 tablespoon sesame oil

1 tablespoon sherry vinegar

1 to 2 teaspoons Asian-style red chili paste

2 cloves garlic, finely minced

Salt and pepper, to taste

Place the dry mustard in a small bowl. Slowly add the water, whisking constantly with a wire whisk to form a smooth emulsion. Add the soy sauce, sesame oil, vinegar, chili paste, garlic, salt, and pepper; mix well. Let stand at room temperature for at least 1 hour before serving, although it's best to store the sauce in a tightly sealed container in the refrigerator for several days before using. Will keep for up to 3 months in the refrigerator, but it is best if used within 1 month.

english cheddar cheese soup with brown mustard and ale

4 tablespoons unsalted butter

4 tablespoons all-purpose flour

1 tablespoon brown mustard seeds

1 teaspoon ground caraway seeds

1/4 cup prepared brown or German-style mustard

2 cups dark ale

6 cups homemade vegetable stock (page 13) or canned vegetable broth (preferably low-sodium)

2 cups whole milk

1 pound sharp English Cheddar cheese, coarsely grated

Salt and pepper, to taste

➤ This hearty soup is satisfying and filling, especially when paired with a pint of ale and dark bread spread with sweet butter.

HOT 2

makes about 6 servings

In a heavy-bottomed, 6-quart pot, melt the butter over moderate heat. Add the flour, mix to form a paste, and cook over moderately low heat 5 to 7 minutes, stirring frequently, until light golden brown. Add the mustard seeds, caraway seeds, and prepared mustard and cook 2 minutes, stirring constantly.

Slowly add the ale, whisking constantly with a wire whisk to form a smooth mixture. Add the vegetable stock and milk and bring to a boil over high heat, whisking constantly to prevent lumps from forming. Boil for 25 to 30 minutes, stirring occasionally, until the mixture is slightly thick and no lumps remain. (If there are any lumps at this point, strain through a fine wire mesh or sieve and return to the pan.)

Add the cheese, stirring constantly until thoroughly melted, about 3 minutes. Remove from the heat, season with salt and pepper, and serve immediately.

1 tablespoon sugar

1 tablespoon prepared hot
Chinese mustard

2 teaspoons Chinese hot
black bean sauce

Salt and pepper, to taste

$^1/_3$ cup cold water

3 tablespoons cornstarch

20 eggroll wrappers

$^3/_4$ to 1 cup vegetable oil,
for frying

To fry the eggrolls: In a 12-inch sauté pan, heat ½ cup of the vegetable oil over moderately high heat. When the oil is hot but not smoking, add 5 or 6 eggrolls. Cook, turning frequently to promote even browning, 1½ to 2 minutes, or until all sides are golden brown. Remove with tongs or a slotted spoon and drain on paper towels. Cook the remaining eggrolls in this fashion, adding more oil as needed. Serve immediately with the mustard dipping sauce.

east indian pickled mangoes with mustard seed

3 cups white vinegar

2 tablespoons coarsely
ground yellow mustard
seeds

1 tablespoon whole brown
mustard seeds

3 cloves garlic, thinly sliced

$^1/_4$ cup dark molasses

2 tablespoons kosher salt

2 large green mangoes
(about 1½ pounds), halved,
pitted, and cut into $^1/_4$-inch
wedges

➤ Serve this pungent condiment with a traditional East Indian feast or with grilled vegetables and steamed rice.

To allow time for the pickling process, prepare this condiment at least three weeks before you plan to serve it. Mangoes are usually available year-round, although the peak season in the United States is late spring through summer.

HOTTER 5
makes 10 to 12 servings

In a 4-quart saucepan, combine the vinegar, mustard, garlic, molasses, and salt. Bring to a boil over high heat and cook 15 minutes, stirring occasionally. Add the mango and cook 5 to 7 minutes, or until tender. Remove from the heat and cool to room temperature. Transfer to a nonreactive container with a tight-fitting lid and store in the refrigerator for at least 3 weeks before serving. Will keep in the refrigerator for up to 2 months.

root vegetable slaw with creamy mustard dressing

Place the beets in a small saucepan and cover with cold water. Bring to a boil over high heat, reduce the heat to moderate, cover, and cook 40 to 45 minutes, or until tender when pierced with a fork. Drain and cool to room temperature. Remove skins and cut into slivers. Set aside.

Blanch the carrots and celery root in a pot of boiling water. Drain well and refresh in cold water. Dry thoroughly and set aside.

In a large bowl, whisk together the olive oil, mustards, and honey to form a smooth mixture. Slowly add the vinegar and whisk to form a smooth emulsion. Add the coriander, parsley, and reserved carrots and celery root. Toss gently and season with salt and pepper. Just before serving, add the beets and walnuts; mix gently *just* until combined (avoid overmixing, lest the beets turn the entire mixture red). Serve on a bed of mustard greens.

➤ The contrasting flavors and colors of beets, carrots, and celery root combine to make a visually stunning, tasty, and healthful salad. Paired with rye crackers and Swiss cheese, this dish makes a fine autumn lunch.

HOTTEST 7

makes 4 to 6 servings

5 small beets, trimmed

3 carrots, slivered

2 small celery roots, trimmed, peeled, and slivered

1/2 cup olive oil

2 tablespoons prepared coarse-grained mustard

1 tablespoon prepared jalapeño or hot mustard

1 tablespoon honey

2 tablespoons apple cider vinegar

1 teaspoon ground coriander

1/4 cup finely chopped fresh parsley

Salt and pepper, to taste

1/3 cup coarsely chopped toasted walnuts

Mustard greens, for lining platter

Classic Potato Salad with Mustard Dressing

½ pound thick sliced bacon

1 large onion, cut in small dice

Mustard Dressing:

½ cup Dijon mustard

3 cloves garlic, minced

½ cup olive oil

¼ cup sherry vinegar

1 tablespoon brown mustard seeds

1½ pounds tiny new potatoes, halved

¼ cup capers, drained

1 small red pepper, cut into small triangles

Salt and pepper, to taste

1 small bunch mustard greens, trimmed

Tiny new potatoes, smokey bacon, and assertive mustard form the backbone of this traditional potato salad, but crisp, refreshing red peppers and bright-tasting mustard greens add a startling new twist.
Makes 4 servings.   Hot: rated 3

Cook the bacon in a large skillet until crisp. Remove with a slotted spoon and drain on paper towels. When cool enough to handle, chop coarsely and place in a large bowl. Set aside until needed.

Cook the onion in the remaining bacon fat over moderate heat for 15 minutes. Remove with a slotted spoon and add to the bacon.

To make the Mustard Dressing: Place the mustard and garlic in a bowl; mix well. Using a wire whisk, incorporate the olive oil a bit at a time, whisking all the while to form a smooth emulsion. Add the vinegar and whisk until smooth. Add the mustard seeds and mix well.

Meanwhile, cook the potatoes in salted boiling water until they are tender but not mushy. Drain in a colander and cool slightly. Add the potatoes to the bacon and onion and mix gently. Add the dressing, capers, and red pepper, and mix gently. Season with salt and pepper and serve on a bed of mustard greens.

Caramelized Onion-Mustard Tart with Gruyère Cheese

LONG, SLOW COOKING YIELDS SWEET, MILD-FLAVORED ONIONS THAT COMBINE BEAUTIFULLY WITH THE
NUTTY TASTE OF GRUYÈRE CHEESE, SWEET TOMATOES, AND PUNGENT DRY MUSTARD IN THIS SAVORY TART.

MAKES 6 TO 8 SERVINGS. ~ **HOT #2**

TO MAKE THE TART SHELL: Place the flour, mustard seeds, and salt in a medium bowl and mix well. Using your fingers, mix in the butter, rubbing it against the flour until the mixture resembles coarse meal. Still mixing with your fingers, add just enough ice water to form the mixture into a ball. Flatten into a disc and wrap tightly in plastic. Refrigerate for at least 2 hours or up to 2 days. Remove from the refrigerator 30 minutes before rolling.

Preheat oven to 350° F. Lightly grease a 12-inch tart pan with a removable bottom.

On a lightly floured surface, roll the dough into a circle approximately 14 inches in diameter. Gently fit the dough into the pan, making the edge extend about ¼ inch above the sides of the pan to allow for shrinkage while baking. Cover the bottom and sides of the dough with parchment paper or foil and fill with pie weights or dried beans. Bake for 15 minutes. Remove the pie weights and bake an additional 10 minutes, or until the bottom and sides are light golden brown. Remove from the oven and cool to room temperature. Increase oven temperature to 450° F.

TO MAKE THE FILLING: In a very large sauté pan, cook the onions in the olive oil over high heat for 10 minutes, stirring frequently. Add the garlic, sherry, and thyme and cook 1 minute. Reduce the heat to moderately low and cook 30 to 35 minutes, stirring frequently, until the onions are very soft, golden brown, and sweet. Remove from the heat and transfer to a bowl. When cool, add the Coleman's mustard and cheese and mix well. Season with salt and pepper. Arrange the filling in the tart shell, making an

TART SHELL:

1¾ cups all-purpose flour

1 tablespoon yellow mustard seeds

2 teaspoons kosher or sea salt

6 tablespoons unsalted butter, cut into very small pieces

4 to 5 tablespoons ice water

FILLING:

4 very large onions, quartered and cut into ¼-inch-wide wedges

3 tablespoons olive oil

3 cloves garlic, finely chopped

½ cup dry sherry

1 teaspoon dried thyme

¼ cup Coleman's dry mustard

½ pound imported Gruyère cheese, finely grated

Salt and pepper, to taste

2 small tomatoes, cut into ⅛-inch-thick slices

---

even layer all the way to the edges. Evenly cover with the tomato slices.

Bake on the top shelf of the oven for 12 or 13 minutes, or until the filling is hot and the tomatoes are wilted. Remove from the oven and cool slightly before cutting into wedges to serve.

Creamy Mustard, Potato, and Leek Gratin

COLEMAN'S MUSTARD POWDER AND WHOLE YELLOW MUSTARD SEEDS ADD DEPTH AND TEXTURE TO THIS CLASSIC POTATO DISH.
RICH, CREAMY, AND ROBUST IN FLAVOR, THE GRATIN PAIRS WELL WITH GRILLED STEAKS OR LAMB, OR WITH ROASTED CHICKEN.
FOR A SATISFYING VEGETARIAN MEAL, SERVE THE WARM GRATIN ON A BED OF MIXED BABY GREENS AND ACCOMPANY WITH HOT ROLLS.

MAKES ABOUT 8 SERVINGS. ～ **HOT #1**

Preheat oven to 375° F. Lightly grease a 9-by-12-inch baking pan.

In a large sauté pan, cook the leeks, garlic, and mustard seeds in the butter over moderately high heat for 5 minutes, stirring frequently. Set aside.

Arrange one third of the potatoes in a single layer on the bottom of the baking pan; evenly distribute one half of the leek mixture over the top. Arrange half of the remaining potatoes over the leeks, making an even layer. Cover with the remaining leeks. Make the final layer using the remaining potatoes.

Place the Coleman's mustard in a medium bowl. Slowly add the cream a little at a time, whisking with a wire whisk to form a smooth mixture. Season with salt and pepper. Slowly pour the mustard cream over the potatoes. Bake on the middle rack of the oven for 1½ hours, or until the potatoes are very tender and the sauce is very thick. Remove from the oven and let stand at room temperature for 7 to 10 minutes before cutting into squares. Serve immediately.

2 large leeks, trimmed (white part only) halved, and thinly sliced

2 cloves garlic, finely chopped

1½ tablespoons yellow mustard seeds

3 tablespoons unsalted butter

6 large baking potatoes, peeled, halved, and cut into ¼-inch-thick slices

⅓ cup Coleman's dry mustard

2 cups heavy cream

Salt and pepper, to taste

braised winter vegetables with lemon-mustard sauce

In a large pot, bring 1 quart of salted water to boil over high heat. Add the onions and return to the boil. Reduce the heat to moderately high and cook 9 or 10 minutes, or until they are tender but not mushy. Drain immediately and cool to room temperature. When cool enough to handle, remove the skins and trim root ends. Set aside until needed.

In a shallow-sided skillet, cook the carrots, turnips, and mustard seeds in the olive oil and butter over moderate heat 10 minutes, stirring occasionally. Add the reserved onions, vegetable stock, prepared mustard, lemon juice, and lemon zest and mix well. Cook 3 to 4 minutes, stirring frequently, until the vegetables are coated with the sauce. Season with salt and pepper and serve immediately, garnished with minced parsley.

➤ Although this vegetable dish looks and tastes rich and creamy, the piquant sauce is made with only one tablespoon of butter—and no cream.

HOT 1

makes 4 to 6 servings

8 small pearl onions, trimmed and peeled

3 carrots, trimmed and cut on the diagonal into 3/4-inch-long pieces

2 turnips, trimmed, quartered, and cut into 3/4-inch wedges

1 tablespoon yellow mustard seeds

2 tablespoons olive oil

1 tablespoon unsalted butter

1/2 cup homemade vegetable stock (page 13) or canned vegetable broth (preferably low-sodium)

1/4 cup prepared champagne or Dijon mustard

2 tablespoons fresh lemon juice

Grated zest from 1 lemon

Salt and pepper, to taste

1/4 cup minced fresh parsley, for garnish (optional)

baked mustard-molasses black-eyed peas

1 large onion, cut into small dice

3 cloves garlic, minced

1 1/2 tablespoons peanut or vegetable oil

3 cups cooked black-eyed peas

2/3 cup prepared Gulden's or other yellow mustard

1/4 cup dark molasses

2 1/2 tablespoons unsalted butter, cut into small pieces

2 tablespoons mustard powder

2 1/2 tablespoons red wine vinegar

Salt and pepper, to taste

➤ Present this rustic American-style dish for supper on a wintery evening with a green salad of mild and bitter greens and black bread and butter. Mugs of Oktoberfest beer would top it off perfectly.

HOT 2

makes 4 to 6 servings

Preheat oven to 375° F.

In a large sauté pan, cook the onion and garlic in the oil over moderate heat 7 or 8 minutes, or until light golden brown. Transfer to a 1½-quart ovenproof casserole. Add the cooked black-eyed peas, prepared mustard, molasses, butter, mustard powder, and red wine vinegar. Mix well and season with salt and pepper. Cover with foil and bake in the center of the oven 30 minutes. Remove foil and bake on upper shelf of oven 10 to 15 minutes, or until edges and top are bubbling and toasty brown. Serve immediately.

mustard-glazed wild mushroom ragoût

3/4 **pound portobello mushrooms, stemmed and cut into** 1/2**-inch pieces**

3/4 **pound domestic brown or button mushrooms, stemmed and quartered**

3 **tablespoons olive oil**

1 **tablespoon unsalted butter**

3 **shallots, thinly sliced**

3 **cloves garlic, minced**

1 1/2 **teaspoons dried thyme**

1 **teaspoon rubbed sage**

1/3 **pound shiitake mushrooms, stemmed and cut into** 1/2**-inch pieces**

1/4 **pound medium oyster mushrooms, halved**

1/3 **cup dry sherry**

1/4 **cup mushroom soy sauce**

1/4 **cup prepared Dijon mustard**

2 **tablespoons prepared champagne mustard or other mild mustard**

3 **tablespoons half-and-half**

Salt and pepper, to taste

1/4 **cup minced fresh parsley, for garnish**

➤ This elegant mushroom dish goes together quickly and easily. It makes an outstanding companion to grilled polenta, mixed white and wild rices, mashed potatoes, or cooked pasta.

HOT 1

makes 4 to 6 servings

In a large, nonstick sauté pan, cook the portobello and brown mushrooms in 2 tablespoons of the olive oil over moderately high heat, stirring occasionally, until any liquid has evaporated and the mushrooms are very light golden brown. Remove from the pan and transfer to a bowl. Set aside.

In the same pan, heat the remaining tablespoon of olive oil and the butter. Add the shallots, garlic, herbs, and shiitake and oyster mushrooms and cook over moderate heat, stirring occasionally, until shallots and mushrooms are tender. Add the reserved mushrooms, the sherry, soy sauce, mustards, and half-and-half. Mix gently and cook 6 or 7 minutes, stirring occasionally, until mixture is slightly thick and aromatic.

Season with salt and pepper, garnish with parsley, and serve immediately.

Indian Lentils with Brown Mustard Seeds and Mango

This traditional Indian lentil dish gets heat from both mustard seeds and prepared mustard. The slightly sweet flavor and velvety texture of the mango adds an uncommon and welcome flavor to the spicy lentils. Serve with basmati rice and chutney and two or three vegetable side dishes for a vegetarian meal, or serve with roasted meats or poultry.
Makes 4 to 6 servings.   *Hotter: rated 4*

2 medium onions, cut in small dice

4 cloves garlic, thinly sliced

½ cup brown mustard seeds

2 teaspoons each ground cumin and coriander

1 teaspoon each ground fennel seed, anise seed, and fenugreek

3 tablespoons olive oil

3 tablespoons unsalted butter

1½ cups brown lentils, sorted

1½ quarts water

2 large mangoes, peeled and seeded, cut in small dice

¼ cup prepared hot English mustard

Salt and pepper, to taste

¾ cup chopped cilantro leaves

Cook the onion, garlic, mustard seeds, and spices in the olive oil and butter over high heat for 5 minutes, stirring frequently. Set aside until needed.

Meanwhile, place the lentils and water in a large pot. Bring to a boil over high heat. Reduce the heat to moderate, add the onion spice mixture, and mix well. Simmer for 45 minutes or until the lentils are tender and the mixture is slightly soupy. Add the mango and mustard, season with salt and pepper and garnish with the cilantro. Serve immediately.

Mustard- and Honey-Braised Brussels Sprouts

EVEN THOSE USUALLY DISINTERESTED IN BRUSSELS SPROUTS MAY BE TEMPTED BY THESE MUSTARD- AND HONEY-GLAZED VEGETABLES. THIS AUTUMNAL SIDE DISH COMPLEMENTS ROASTED POULTRY AND FRESH PORK OR HAM.

MAKES ABOUT 6 SERVINGS. ∾ **HOT #1**

⅓ cup Dijon mustard

1½ tablespoons honey

3 shallots, halved and thinly sliced

2 cloves garlic, finely chopped

2 tablespoons unsalted butter

1 tablespoon olive oil

½ cup dry sherry

1½ pounds Brussels sprouts, trimmed and halved

1 cup homemade chicken stock or low-sodium chicken broth

Salt and pepper, to taste

In a small bowl, combine the mustard and honey. Set aside.

In a large sauté pan, cook the shallots and garlic in the butter and oil over moderate heat for 3 minutes, stirring frequently. Add the sherry and cook 5 minutes, or until it has almost evaporated.

Add the Brussels sprouts and chicken broth to the sauté pan and bring to a boil over high heat. Reduce the heat to moderate, cover with a tight-fitting lid, and cook 13 to 15 minutes, or until the sprouts are tender. Remove the lid, add the mustard-honey mixture and cook 1 to 2 minutes over high heat, stirring frequently, until the sauce coats the vegetables and is heated through. Season with salt and pepper and serve immediately.

cabbage rolls with mustard-spiked vegetables

To prepare the cabbage leaves: Fill with salted water a pot large enough to accommodate the entire head of cabbage. Bring to a boil over high heat. Drop the head of cabbage in the boiling water for about 1 minute, or until the outer leaves are soft and pliable. Remove the entire head from the water, and gently remove as many of the outer leaves as possible without tearing them. Return the head to the water and repeat the process until you have 12 to 15 whole leaves without any tears. At the bottom of each leaf, cut a 'V' shape to remove the tough, fibrous vein.

If the leaves are not pliable enough to mold around the filling and form into rolls, drop individually into the boiling water and cook 20 to 30 seconds or until pliable but not overcooked and too soft. Drain between layers of paper towels. Set aside until needed.

To make the filling: In a very large sauté pan, cook the onion, garlic, mustard seeds, and spices in the *ghee* over high heat 3 minutes, stirring frequently, until the spices are aromatic. Add the water and cook 3 minutes, stirring frequently. Add the carrot, tomatoes, and chickpeas and bring to a boil. Reduce the heat to moderately low and cook, stirring occasionally, 35 to 40 minutes, or until all the vegetables are tender and the mixture is thick. Remove from the heat and cool slightly. Add the prepared mustard and season with salt and pepper; mix well.

To make the cabbage rolls: Preheat oven to 400° F. Lightly grease a 9-x-12-inch baking pan. Place the cabbage leaves on a flat surface, with the V-shaped cuts closest to you. Close the triangle by bringing the cut corners of the cabbage leaf together to form an unbroken circle. Along the bottom of the leaf, place 2 to 3 tablespoons of the filling.

(continued overleaf)

➤ The filling for these zesty cabbage rolls may be made one or two days in advance and refrigerated until ready to use.

Loaded with nutrition and packed with flavor, these rolls are terrific served with a smooth tomato sauce or drizzled with plain yogurt.

HOT 2

makes about 12 rolls; 6 servings

1 very large head white cabbage, cored

1 large onion, finely chopped

3 cloves garlic, finely chopped

2 tablespoons brown mustard seeds

1 tablespoon ground cumin

2 teaspoons *each* ground coriander, fenugreek, fennel seeds, and turmeric

1/2 teaspoon *each* ground cloves and caraway seeds

3 tablespoons *ghee* or vegetable oil (see note, p.53)

1/2 cup water

1 small carrot, finely diced

2 cups peeled, seeded, and finely chopped tomatoes

1 1/2 cups cooked chickpeas, coarsely chopped, plus 1 cup whole cooked chickpeas

3 tablespoons prepared brown mustard

Salt and pepper, to taste

Begin rolling, folding the sides of the leaf in over the filling as you go, forming a neat, tight roll. Assemble the remaining leaves and filling in this fashion, taking care to completely enclose the filling within the leaves. Place in the prepared pan, cover tightly with tinfoil, and bake 10 to 12 minutes, or until the rolls are heated through. Serve immediately with additional mustard on the side, if desired.

mustard-glazed pumpkin wedges

1 tablespoon softened unsalted butter, cut into 4 pieces

¹/₃ cup dry sherry

¹/₄ cup Dijon mustard

¹/₄ cup whole milk

3 ¹/₂ tablespoons brown mustard seeds

2 teaspoons ground coriander

2 tablespoons peanut oil

1 small eating pumpkin (about 1 pound), peeled, seeded, and cut into ¹/₂-inch-thick wedges (18 to 20 wedges)

Splash sherry vinegar or apple cider vinegar

Salt and pepper, to taste

➤ Serve this savory vegetable side dish with a salad of mixed baby greens tossed with pears and garnished with toasted walnuts and blue cheese. Warm rolls and butter, or even a basket of interesting crackers, would complete the meal.

HOT 1

makes about 6 servings

In a small bowl, combine the butter, sherry, Dijon mustard, milk, mustard seeds, and coriander. Mix until well combined; set aside.

In a very large, nonstick sauté pan, heat the peanut oil over moderate heat until warm. Add the pumpkin wedges and cook, stirring frequently, 5 to 7 minutes, or until light golden brown on all sides. Add the sherry-mustard mixture and cook 4 or 5 minutes, stirring gently, until the pumpkin is tender and the sauce is thick and aromatic. Add the vinegar and season with salt and pepper. Serve immediately.

Baked Macaroni with Mustard and Cheddar Cheese

A HEALTHY DOSE OF DIJON MUSTARD AND WHOLE YELLOW MUSTARD SEEDS ADDS AN ADDITIONAL LAYER
OF FLAVOR AND TEXTURE TO THIS AMERICAN CLASSIC. WHILE TERRIFIC AS A MAIN DISH,
IT ALSO GOES WELL WITH BAKED HAM OR PORK CHOPS OR WITH ROASTED OR SMOKED POULTRY.
MAKES 6 TO 8 SERVINGS. ⌒ **HOT #2**

¾ *pound elbow macaroni pasta*

2 tablespoons unsalted butter

¼ cup all-purpose flour

1½ tablespoons yellow mustard seeds

1 teaspoon ground cumin

2 cups half-and-half, warmed

½ cup whole milk, warmed

¾ *pound sharp yellow cheddar cheese, coarsely grated*

⅓ cup Dijon mustard

Salt and pepper, to taste

Preheat oven to 400° F. Generously grease a round, deep-sided, 4-quart baking dish.

In a 10-quart pot, bring 7 quarts of salted water to boil over high heat. Add the macaroni, stir vigorously, and return to a boil. Cook 7 minutes, stirring occasionally, until almost al dente. Drain well in a colander and place in a large bowl. Cover with a damp kitchen towel or place a piece of plastic wrap directly on top of the pasta. Set aside.

In 3-quart, heavy-bottomed saucepan, melt the butter over moderately low heat. Add the flour, mustard seeds, and cumin and mix well. Cook 7 or 8 minutes, stirring frequently, until the mixture is very pale brown and smells nutty.

Slowly add about ¾ cup of the half-and-half, whisking constantly with a wire whisk to prevent lumps from forming and to make a smooth emulsion. Slowly add the remaining half-and-half, whisking constantly to avoid forming lumps. When all the cream has been added, add the milk and mix well, scraping the bottom of the pan with a wooden spoon. Bring to a boil over high heat and cook 2 minutes, whisking constantly. Reduce the heat to moderate and cook 10 to 12 minutes, stirring frequently to prevent the bottom from scorching. Remove from the heat. (If the sauce has any lumps, press the mixture through a fine wire sieve into a large bowl; return the strained mixture to the saucepan.) Add three fourths of the cheese to the hot cream mixture and stir until thoroughly melted. Add the mustard and mix well.

Add the cream mixture to the macaroni and toss gently. Season with salt and pepper and turn into the prepared baking dish. Bake on the bottom shelf of the oven for 20 minutes, or until the center is piping hot. Evenly distribute the remaining cheese over the top and return to the top shelf of the oven. Bake 5 minutes longer, or until the cheese is melted and starting to bubble. Remove from the oven and serve immediately.

triple-mustard mushroom fritters

In a large bowl, combine the flour, mustard powder, baking powder, and mustard seeds; mix well and set aside.

In a small bowl, whisk together the butter, egg yolks (refrigerate the whites until ready to use), garlic, Dijon mustard, sage, salt, and pepper. Slowly add the milk, whisking constantly to form a smooth emulsion. Add to the dry ingredients, whisking constantly to form a smooth mixture. (You may switch to a wooden spoon once the two components are thoroughly combined.)

Cover with plastic and refrigerate for at least 4 hours or overnight.

Just before cooking, beat the egg whites until stiff but not dry. Fold the whites into the batter and stir gently until *just* mixed.

In a large, heavy-bottomed saucepan, heat 4 inches of oil over moderately high heat until hot but not smoking. Select as many mushrooms as will comfortably fit in one layer in the oil-filled saucepan, and drop them into the batter. Make sure each mushroom is completely covered with the batter as you remove them with a slotted spoon or tongs. Drop immediately into the hot oil and cook, turning as needed, until well browned on all sides and slightly puffy. Remove with a slotted spoon and drain on paper towels. Let the oil come back up to the proper temperature before adding another batch of mushrooms. Cook the remaining mushrooms in this fashion, adding more oil as needed. Serve immediately, garnished with lemon wedges.

➤ Don't let the long ingredient list or seemingly complicated instructions frighten you away. The fritters are quite simple to prepare and cook, and the results are sensational. They make an outstanding hors d'oeuvre for cocktail parties or a formal dinner.

HOT 2

makes about 6 servings

1 1/4 cups all-purpose flour

2 tablespoons mustard powder

1/2 teaspoon baking powder

1 1/2 tablespoons yellow mustard seeds

3 tablespoons unsalted butter, melted and cooled to room temperature

2 eggs, separated

2 cloves garlic, minced

2 tablespoons prepared Dijon mustard

1 teaspoon rubbed sage

1 teaspoon kosher salt

1/2 teaspoon black pepper

1 cup whole milk

3 to 4 cups vegetable oil, for cooking

1 pound small button mushrooms, wiped clean and trimmed

Lemon wedges, for garnish

rigatoni with broccoli, peppers, and creamy mustard sauce

5 cloves garlic, finely chopped

1 1/2 tablespoons olive oil

3 cups heavy cream

1 teaspoon dried thyme

1 large red bell pepper, cut into 3/4-inch-long rectangles or triangles

3 tablespoons prepared Dijon mustard

3 tablespoons prepared coarse-grained mustard

1 pound rigatoni pasta

3 cups broccoli flowerettes

1 cup toasted walnuts, coarsely chopped

Salt and pepper, to taste

➤ This luscious, cream-based pasta dish is a comforting indulgence that will satisfy cravings for something special. Accompany with a crisp sauvignon blanc or chenin blanc and warm, crusty bread.

HOT 2

makes about 6 servings

In a 12-quart pot, bring 8 quarts salted water to a boil over high heat.

Meanwhile, in a large sauté pan, cook the garlic in the olive oil over moderately low heat 5 minutes, or until very light golden brown. Add the cream and thyme and cook about 15 minutes, stirring frequently to prevent the mixture from boiling over. Add the bell pepper and mustards; mix well and remove from the heat.

Add the rigatoni to the boiling water, return to the boil, and stir well. Cook over high heat 12 minutes, or until pasta is *al dente*. Add the broccoli flowerettes and cook 20 seconds longer. Immediately drain in a colander and shake until no water remains. Place in a very large, preheated bowl and cover with a kitchen towel.

Reheat the cream mixture over high heat 2 to 3 minutes, stirring constantly, until the mixture is hot and bubbling and the pepper is crisp-tender. Immediately add to the pasta and broccoli, along with the walnuts, and toss gently. Season with salt and pepper and serve immediately.

White Bean–Smoked Chicken Salad with Mustard

This Tuscan-style white bean salad is ideal for a spring or summer picnic. Use a vegetable peeler to make thin shavings of Parmesan cheese for the garnish. To easily cut smoked turkey into small cubes, ask your butcher or deli person to make one thick slice for you.
Makes 4 servings.   Hot: rated 3

Soak the beans in plenty of water for 8 hours or overnight. Drain the beans and place them in a saucepan with the bay leaves. Add 2 quarts of fresh water and bring to a boil over high heat. Reduce the heat to moderately high, and cook for 45 minutes to 1 hour or until the beans are very tender but not mushy. (Meanwhile make the vinaigrette.) Drain and place in a large bowl. Add the smoked chicken and onion and mix gently.

To make the vinaigrette: Place the mustard and garlic in a bowl; mix well. Using a wire whisk, incorporate the olive oil and then the vinegar a little at a time, whisking to form a smooth emulsion. Add the mustard seeds, herbs, and salt and pepper; mix well.

Dress the salad with the vinaigrette and mix gently. Serve at room temperature on a bed of radicchio or inside big individual leaves, garnished with shavings of Parmesan cheese and rosemary sprigs.

1½ cups white navy beans, sorted

2 quarts water

2 bay leaves

1 cup diced smoked chicken or turkey (about ½ pound)

1 small red onion, halved and thinly sliced

Vinaigrette:

¼ cup Dijon mustard

2 cloves garlic, minced

¾ cup olive oil

⅓ cup sherry vinegar

2 tablespoons yellow mustard seeds

2 teaspoons each dried rosemary, thyme, and sage

Salt and pepper, to taste

1 large head radicchio, trimmed

2 ounces Parmesan cheese

Rosemary sprigs, for garnish

Ham and Rice Salad with Two Mustards

THIS COLORFUL SALAD IS SIMPLE TO PREPARE AND TRAVELS WELL,
MAKING IT AN IDEAL SUMMER BARBECUE OR PICNIC DISH.
MAKES ABOUT 6 SERVINGS. ◦⌒ HOT #2

¼ cup olive oil

¼ cup peanut or vegetable oil

3 tablespoons red wine vinegar

3 tablespoons white wine mustard or
   champagne mustard

1 tablespoon honey

2 cloves garlic, minced

½ teaspoon each ground coriander, fennel seeds,
   and cumin

1½ cups long-grain brown rice

Two ¼-inch-thick slices smoked ham
   (about ⅔ pound), finely chopped

1 red bell pepper, stemmed, seeded, and cut into
   small dice

1½ cups finely chopped mustard greens

Salt and pepper, to taste

Large mustard green leaves, for lining platter

Place the olive and peanut oils in a small bowl. Slowly add the vinegar, whisking constantly with a wire whisk to form a smooth emulsion. Add the mustard, honey, garlic, and spices and whisk until thoroughly incorporated. Set the dressing aside.

Bring 3 quarts of water to boil over high heat in an 8-quart pot. Add the rice, stir well, and return to a boil. Reduce the heat to moderately high and cook 35 to 40 minutes, or until the rice is al dente. Drain well in fine-sieved colander and place in a large bowl. Cool slightly.

Add the ham, bell pepper, and dressing to the rice; toss well. When the mixture is completely cool, add the mustard greens and mix well. Season with salt and pepper. Serve slightly chilled or at room temperature on a platter lined with the mustard green leaves.

10 large shallots, trimmed
and peeled

10 whole (peeled) cloves garlic

1½ tablespoons yellow
mustard seeds

¼ cup olive oil or
bacon fat

2 bay leaves

2 teaspoons each dried
thyme and rosemary

1 cup white wine

8 small new potatoes, halved

1 large bunch small carrots,
trimmed and peeled

2 cups unsalted beef stock or
broth

¾ pound smoked sausage,
cut into 1-inch pieces

¾ cup Dijon mustard

Salt and pepper, to taste

1 cup chopped parsley,
for garnish

Country-Style French Sausage Ragout with Mustard

Flavorful yet simple, this herb-scented ragout takes less than an hour to prepare. It makes a terrific cold-weather supper served with a salad of bitter greens. Makes 4 servings.   *Hot: rated 2*

In a shallow pot, cook the shallots, garlic, and mustard seeds in the olive oil over moderate heat for 10 minutes, stirring occasionally. Add the herbs and wine and bring to a boil over high heat. Cook for 5 minutes, or until the liquid evaporates. Add the potatoes, carrots, and beef broth; return to a boil. Reduce the heat to moderate and cook for 20 minutes or until the vegetables are almost tender.

Add the sausage and mustard and cook for 5 to 7 minutes, or until the sauce is thick and the sausage is hot all the way through. Season with salt and pepper and garnish with chopped parsley.

Irene's Mustard-Glazed Ham Loaf

VARYING SLIGHTLY FROM MY MOM'S HAM LOAF, THIS RENDITION CALLS FOR BOTH DRY MUSTARD AND WHOLE MUSTARD SEEDS. TO MAKE A COMPLETE MEAL, PAIR THIS SATISFYING MEAT LOAF WITH A GREEN SALAD OR BRAISED CABBAGE, AND SWEET POTATOES OR LENTILS. PASS AN ASSORTMENT OF MUSTARDS TO SATISFY THOSE WHO SIMPLY CAN'T GET ENOUGH OF THE STUFF.

If freshly ground pork and smoked ham are not readily available in your market, you can grind the meat yourself using a food processor or meat grinder.

MAKES 6 TO 8 SERVINGS. ⁓ **HOT #2**

3 tablespoons light brown sugar

3 tablespoons Coleman's dry mustard

3 tablespoons apple cider vinegar

1 pound finely ground boneless smoked ham

1 pound finely ground fresh lean pork shoulder

1 cup finely ground Ritz crackers

3 tablespoons whole yellow mustard seeds

1 teaspoon black pepper

2 eggs, lightly beaten

¾ cup whole milk

Preheat oven to 350° F. Lightly grease an 8½-by-4½-inch loaf pan.

To make the glaze, in a small bowl combine the brown sugar, dry mustard, and vinegar to form a smooth mixture. Set aside.

In a large bowl, place the ham, pork, crackers, mustard seeds, pepper, eggs, and milk. Using your fingers, gently mix the ingredients until just combined. Do not overmix. Transfer the mixture to the prepared loaf pan and smooth the top. Using a sharp fork, poke holes into the entire surface of the ham loaf. Bake on the lower shelf of the oven for 35 minutes.

Remove the ham loaf from the oven and carefully pour the glaze over the top, making sure it goes into the meat rather than over the sides of the pan! Return to the oven and bake on the top shelf 10 to 12 minutes, or until the glaze is hot and several shades darker. Let stand at room temperature for 10 minutes before cutting into 1-inch-thick slices. Serve immediately.

1 2-pound rack of lamb, trimmed of excess fat and ready to carve

¾ cup fine dried bread crumbs

¼ cup Dijon mustard

¼ cup honey mustard

¼ cup yellow mustard seeds

2 tablespoons brown mustard seeds

4 cloves garlic, minced

1 tablespoon dried rosemary

¼ cup minced parsley

Juice from 1 lemon

Rosemary sprigs, for garnish

Honey Mustard:

½ cup Colman's mustard powder

2 tablespoons brown mustard seeds

3 tablespoons dry sherry

⅓ cup honey

Salt and pepper, to taste

Marinade:

¼ cup olive oil

3 cloves garlic, minced

Roast Lamb with Mustard Crust

Serve this elegant dish with roasted potatoes, or polenta and asparagus, or sautéed Swiss chard for a special occasion. A good bottle of zinfandel or cabernet sauvignon would be a splendid addition.
Makes 4 servings.   Hot: rated 2

Preheat oven to 450° F.

Pat the lamb dry with a kitchen towel. Combine the remaining ingredients except the rosemary sprigs in a bowl; mix well. Coat the lamb with the mixture, taking care to cover all sides equally and evenly. Set lamb on a flat roasting rack inside a lightly greased baking pan.

Roast the meat for 15 to 20 minutes, or until medium rare. Remove from the oven and let stand at room temperature for 5 to 7 minutes before slicing. Garnish with the rosemary and serve immediately.

Honey-Mustard Marinated Grilled Pork Tenderloin

You can use commercial honey mustard for this marinade, but I have included a recipe for making your own at home. It is simple and delicious, and making your own mustard is sure to impress your family and friends. Served with sweet potatoes wrapped in foil and cooked in warm coals, and green vegetables, corn, or a salad, this entrée is very easy to make and serve.
Makes 4 servings.   Hot: rated 2

To make the Honey Mustard: Place the Colman's mustard, mustard seeds, sherry, and honey in a small bowl; mix well until smooth. Cover with plastic and let sit at room temperature for 1 to 8 hours before tasting. Mix again and season with salt and pepper. Set aside until needed.

To make the marinade: Place the olive oil, garlic, mustard seeds, and coriander in a bowl. Use a wire whisk to incorporate the wine a bit at

3 tablespoons yellow mustard seeds

1 tablespoon ground coriander

¼ cup dry white wine

¾ cup **Honey Mustard**

1 pork tenderloin (about 1 pound), trimmed of excess fat

a time, whisking all while. Add the mustard, a bit at a time, and mix well to form a smooth emulsion.

Place the tenderloin in a plastic bag with the marinade, making sure that the marinade comes in contact with all sides of the meat. Marinate in the refrigerator for 4 hours or up to 2 days, rotating every 8 hours or so, or at room temperature for 1½ hours.

Prepare a charcoal grill. When it is medium hot (a light coating of gray ash will cover the coals), place the meat on the grill. Cook 12 to 15 minutes, brushing with the marinade as the tenderloin cooks. Do not overcook the meat or it will be tough and dry—it should be barely pink in the center. Remove from the grill and let stand at room temperature for 5 minutes before slicing into ¾-inch rounds.

Chicken Breasts in Mustard Cream Sauce

This rich chicken dish is excellent served with wild rice, or over pasta. Definitely a crowd pleaser, this entrée also requires only a few steps. Sautéed or steamed vegetables will complete the meal.
Makes 4 servings.   *Hot: rated 1*

4 medium-sized chicken breasts

3 cups heavy cream

2 cloves garlic, minced

2 tablespoons brown mustard seeds

1 teaspoon dried thyme

3 tablespoons Dijon mustard

3 tablespoons coarse-grained mustard

Salt and pepper, to taste

Parsley or fresh thyme, for garnish

Place the chicken breasts in a large pot and cover with water. Bring to a boil over high heat; boil for 10 minutes. Remove pot from the heat and let chicken stand for 10 minutes. Remove with a slotted spoon and cool slightly. When cool enough to handle, remove the meat from the bones, taking care to remove the tendons and fat. Set aside until needed.

In a 12- or 15-inch skillet, combine the cream, garlic, mustard seeds, and thyme. Bring to a boil over high heat, stirring constantly since heavy cream cooked over high heat tends to boil over. Cook for 8 to 10 minutes or until the cream is almost thick enough to coat the back of a spoon.

Add the reserved chicken and the mustards and mix well. Cook for 2 to 3 minutes or until the sauce is thick and the chicken is hot all the way through. Season with salt and pepper and garnish with parsley or thyme sprigs. Serve immediately.

Sardine and Coarse-Grained Mustard Sandwiches

Coarse-Grained Mustard:

⅓ cup yellow mustard seeds

2 tablespoons Colman's dry mustard powder

2 tablespoons apple cider vinegar

2 tablespoons water

3 tablespoons olive or vegetable oil

¼ cup soy sauce

2 teaspoons turmeric

Salt and pepper, to taste

4 to 5 tins sardines packed in oil

8 thick slices country-style rye, sourdough, or wheat bread

Escarole, frisée, curly endive, or leafy greens

¾ pound Havarti, Danbo, Gruyère, or any flavorful German or Danish cheese, thinly sliced

Spicy-hot mustard and pleasantly oily sardines are an ideal pairing. Choose a rustic, dense, and flavorful bread for this satisfying lunch or light supper dish, and serve it with ale or stout. You can use fresh sardines if you can find them, but the tinned variety is really quite tasty. Use your favorite commercial coarse-grained mustard if you don't want to make your own. If you would like to serve these sandwiches open-faced, use only 4 slices of bread, and follow the assembly directions for the regular sandwich, leaving off the last piece of bread.
Makes 4 sandwiches. *Hot: rated 3*

To make the Coarse-Grained Mustard: Place all the ingredients except the salt and pepper in a blender. Purée until well blended and the mixture forms a coarse paste. Season with salt and pepper and let stand, covered, at room temperature for 8 hours before using. The mustard improves and becomes less biting as it stands. Four or five days in the refrigerator will make the mustard milder.

Drain the sardines. Spread each slice of bread with the mustard. Arrange some greens on 4 slices of bread, top with a few slices of cheese, and cover with the sardines. Add a bit more greens, and top with the second slice of bread. Slice in half and serve at room temperature.

Grilled Chicken Wings with Two Mustards and Honey

STICKY, GOOEY, AND IRRESISTIBLE, THESE SLIGHTLY SWEET-SAVORY HOT CHICKEN WINGS MAKE
A SENSATIONAL OPENING FOR ANY SUMMER MEAL.

MAKES ABOUT 6 SERVINGS. ᴥ **HOT #2**

½ cup prepared Chinese-style mustard

½ cup Dijon mustard

½ cup honey

2 tablespoons teriyaki sauce

4 cloves garlic, minced

1 teaspoon black pepper

3½ pounds meaty chicken wings

In a bowl large enough to accommodate all the wings, combine the mustards, honey, teriyaki sauce, garlic, and black pepper; mix well, forming a smooth paste. Add the chicken wings and toss well to evenly coat the wings. Cover with foil or plastic and refrigerate for 6 hours or up to 1 day.

Prepare a charcoal grill. When the coals are medium-hot (covered with a thin layer of white ash), place the wings on the grill. Cook, rotating the wings as they brown and brushing them occasionally with the marinade, for 15 to 17 minutes (depending on the heat of the barbecue), or until the exteriors are dark golden brown and crispy and the interiors are cooked through. Remove from the grill and serve immediately.

Melted Cheddar and Sweet Pickle Sandwiches with Two Mustards

A LUNCH COMPOSED ON THIS PIQUANT SANDWICH, A GREEN SALAD, THICK-CUT POTATO CHIPS,
AND A GLASS OF DARK BEER IS SURE TO BRIGHTEN ANY RAINY DAY.
MAKES 4 SERVINGS. ~ **HOT #2**

¼ cup Dijon mustard

¼ cup coarse-grained English or German mustard

⅓ cup finely chopped sweet pickles

4 thick slices dense whole-wheat, light rye,
  or multi-grain bread

½ pound sharp English or Canadian cheddar
  cheese, cut into 16 slices

8 thin tomato slices

Preheat broiler portion of oven.

In a small bowl, combine the mustards and pickles and mix well. Arrange the bread slices on a baking sheet small enough to fit under the broiler. Spread each slice of bread with one fourth of the mustard-pickle mixture and top with the cheese slices, dividing equally. Make sure the cheese is fairly level and the slices extend to the edges of the bread.

Broil in the oven until the cheese is melted and bubbly. Remove from the broiler, top each with tomato slices, and return to the broiler for 1 minute, or until the tomatoes are slightly wilted and warmed through. Serve immediately.

peppercorns

$\mathscr{P}$EPPERCORNS

PEPPER, THE WORLD'S MOST POPULAR SPICE, WAS AT ONE TIME SO UNCOMMON IT WAS CONSIDERED as precious as gold, and in some instances it was used as currency. Nowadays pepper is plentiful and inexpensive; still a valuable spice to the home cook, it is nevertheless taken for granted and unfortunately rarely plays a dominant role.

Native to Indonesia and the tropical forest and equatorial regions of India, pepper is still cultivated in Indonesia and India as well as Malaysia, Brazil, the West Indies, eastern Asia, Cambodia, and Madagascar. *Piper nigrum,* a species of *Piper,* is a climbing plant with 3- to 7-inch heart-shaped green leaves and flowers that bear clustered fruit. Depending on their level of maturity and how they are treated once picked, these fruits eventually come to market as either black, white, or green peppercorns.

BLACK PEPPERCORNS, picked before they fully ripen, are dried in the sun for eight to ten days until they shrink and shrivel and are hard, dry, and black. There are many varieties of black pepper, each with a distinctive taste and aroma. Most popular are Tellicherry and Lampong peppercorns, but well-stocked specialty or spice shops often carry Singapore, Penang, and Alleppey varieties as well.

Traditionally used solely for savory dishes, slightly crushed or whole black peppercorns are beginning to appear in baked goods and other confections. I particularly like pairing dark chocolate with the spice, but it also marries well with such dried fruits as prunes, figs, and dates, as well as such fresh fruits as melon, berries, plums, pears, and figs.

WHITE PEPPERCORNS are picked ripe and then treated to a water bath to remove the outer skins. Once the skin is rubbed off, the inner portion is dried until it turns a pale shade of off-white. In comparison to the black peppercorn, the white variety is smaller and softer, contains a higher percentage of piperine (a heat-lending alkaloid), but fewer aromatic elements, thus rendering it more fiery but less flavorful. The most common types available include Muntok, Sarawak, and Siam.

White peppercorns are good to use when you want a more direct, pointed, and fiery effect rather than one with complex and multilayered characteristics. Although they are normally used in savory dishes, white peppercorns also lend a warm, aromatic, almost fruity flavor to select desserts.

GREEN PEPPERCORNS are picked unripe, but unlike those processed to make black peppercorns, they are immediately freeze-dried or preserved in brine. Less pungent than black or white peppercorns, fruity-tasting green peppercorns are traditionally paired with milder tasting meats, such as chicken, pork and veal, and with fish and seafood. While traveling in Thailand, I sampled several dishes that included small bunches of fresh green peppercorns on the stem—they were extremely pungent!

PINK PEPPERCORNS, technically speaking, are not considered true pepper but rather the dried berries from a South American tree. According to some references, this under-utilized spice is derived from *Shinus terebinthifolius;* others list the source as *Shinus molle.* In any event, pink peppercorns are usually freeze-dried or packed in brine and can be found in specialty food stores or spice shops. Use these aromatic, slightly sweet, distinctive, and pungent peppercorns in cream or butter sauces; with poultry, fish, and seafood; and in desserts that beg for a flowery, spicy flavor followed by a hint of warmth.

When purchasing dried peppercorns, look for whole peppercorns sold in bulk or packed in tightly sealed tubes or containers. To check the freshness, rub a few peppercorns between your fingers and sniff for a pronounced aroma. Black and white pepper are sold preground, but avoid purchasing pepper in this form. Preground pepper often includes fillers and other unwanted ingredients and is usually stale.

I recommend grinding dry peppercorns in a spice or coffee mill for cooking purposes. For the table I prefer an adjustable pepper mill so that the peppercorns can be ground fine, medium, or coarse. A mortar and pestle is convenient for extremely coarse grinding and bruising.

TO BRUISE PEPPERCORNS in a mortar and pestle, place the spice in the center of the mortar and lightly rub with the pestle until the desired texture is achieved. To bruise or grind without a pepper mill, mortar and pestle, or electric grinder, place the spice in a medium-sized bowl and use a smaller bowl that will fit inside it to rub and crush the peppercorns. You can also place the peppercorns on a cutting board and press gently with a heavy skillet or rolling pin until they are bruised. If you try to bruise or crush the peppercorns too aggressively at first they will fly all over the room. Be gentle until they are bruised and then, if desired, you can use more force to grind them smaller.

The recipes in this chapter are undoubtedly among the most unique in this collection. Unlike ginger, mustard, horseradish, and chili peppers, peppercorns are relatively underused and underappreciated, even by seasoned cooks. Classic dishes that highlight this spice are few in number, so I therefore developed recipes that showcase the four distinctly different peppercorns especially for this book.

My favorites in this chapter include *Broccoli and Red Bell Pepper Salad with Black and White Peppercorns; Pasta with Peppered Artichokes, Ham, and Toasted Almonds;* and *Seared Four-Peppercorn Swordfish with Coriander,* all of which contain a moderate amount of heat provided by at least two different peppercorns. More penetrating and fiery are *Peppery Chicken-Fried Rice* and *Poached Chicken Breasts with Peppercorn Sauce.*

In addition to the savory recipes, I have included two unique desserts: *Vanilla Rice Pudding with Green and Pink Peppercorns,* which takes on an almost floral quality from the pepper, and the dusky, intensely flavored *Chocolate-Hazelnut Mousse with Black Pepper,* which generates a warm, spicy effect on the palate.

Whether included in savory or sweet dishes, I hope these recipes will highlight the culinary versatility of this neglected spice.

peppery cheddar cheese crisps

1 1/4 cups all-purpose flour

1/2 cup fine yellow cornmeal

1/2 teaspoon baking powder

2 tablespoons black pepper-corns, coarsely ground

1 teaspoon kosher or sea salt

10 tablespoons (1 1/4 sticks) unsalted butter, cut into small pieces

1/2 pound sharp Cheddar cheese, finely grated

3 to 3 1/2 tablespoons seltzer water

➤ Judging from the speed and enthusiasm with which they are gobbled up every time I make them, I suggest hiding these habit-forming crackers until you're ready to serve them. They're great with a crisp white wine or pale ale.

HOT 3

makes 55 to 60 crackers

Combine the flour, cornmeal, baking powder, black pepper, and salt in a medium bowl; mix well. Add the butter and cheese and, using your fingers, quickly mix them into the dry ingredients until a well-blended dough forms. Add just enough water to form a smooth, pliable dough. Gather into a ball and place on a cutting board.

Divide the ball into four equal pieces and shape each into a ball. Press and roll each into a long cylinder, approximately 1 1/4 inches in diameter. Wrap each cylinder in plastic wrap and refrigerate at least 4 hours or up to 2 days.

Preheat oven to 400° F. Remove the dough from the refrigerator. Using a very sharp knife, cut the dough into 1/8-inch-thick (or thinner, if possible) rounds. (You may want to run the knife under very hot water from time to time to facilitate cutting the dough.) Arrange the rounds on *ungreased* baking sheets, leaving approximately a 3/4-inch space between each one. Bake 7 or 8 minutes until light golden brown, rotating the pans once to encourage even baking. Using a spatula, immediately remove from baking sheets to wire cooling racks. When cool, store in tightly sealed plastic bags or an airtight container at room temperature for up to 4 days.

Avocado Soup with Green Peppercorns

1 medium onion, cut in medium dice

2 cloves garlic, minced

1 tablespoon ground coriander

1 teaspoon ground cumin

¼ cup olive oil

4 large ripe avocados, peeled, pitted, and coarsely chopped

2½ quarts light chicken stock

⅓ cup green peppercorns in brine, drained (reserve a few for garnish)

Salt and pepper, to taste

Cilantro leaves, for garnish

Rich, velvety, and smooth, this spring or summer soup can be served hot or cold, and is delicious with warm tortillas or tortilla chips served with tomato salsa cruda and fresh Mexican cheese. The piquant green peppercorns in brine balance the richness of the avocados and add just the right amount of zing.
Makes about 6 servings.   Hotter: rated 4

In a large saucepan, cook the onion, garlic, and spices in the olive oil over moderate heat for 10 minutes, stirring frequently. Add the avocados and chicken stock and bring to a boil over high heat. Reduce the heat to moderate and cook for 20 minutes. Cool to room temperature.

Purée the soup mixture in a blender until very smooth. Transfer back to the saucepan and bring to a boil over high heat. Add the peppercorns and salt and pepper. Reduce the heat to moderate and cook for 10 minutes. Serve with a garnish of cilantro and a few peppercorns.

Scallop-Corn Chowder with Pink and White Peppercorns

FINELY GROUND WHITE PEPPERCORNS ADD HEAT AND WHOLE PINK PEPPERCORNS LEND A WARM, FLORAL
NOTE TO THIS RICH CHOWDER. TEAM WITH A GREEN SALAD AND WARM DINNER ROLLS FOR A LIGHT SUPPER.
MAKES ABOUT 8 SERVINGS. ∽ **HOT #2**

In a 10-quart, heavy-bottomed saucepan, cook the onion in the peanut oil and butter over moderately high heat for 7 minutes, stirring frequently. Add the white peppercorns, coriander, fennel seeds, and wine and bring to a boil over high heat. Cook, stirring frequently, 3 to 4 minutes, or until the wine is almost evaporated. Add the clam juice, cream, and pink peppercorns and cook 15 minutes, stirring frequently, until the mixture is the consistency of heavy cream.

Add the corn and cook 3 minutes. Add the scallops and cook 1½ to 2 minutes, stirring frequently, or until the scallops are just opaque in the center. Take care not to overcook the scallops. Season with salt and black pepper, if desired. Serve immediately, garnished with the chives.

1 large onion, cut into small dice

2 tablespoons peanut or vegetable oil

1 tablespoon unsalted butter

2 tablespoons coarsely ground white peppercorns

½ tablespoon ground coriander

1 teaspoon ground fennel seeds

¾ cup dry white wine

5 cups clam juice

2½ cups heavy cream

1 tablespoon whole pink peppercorns

2 large ears corn, shaved (about 2 cups fresh corn kernels)

1 pound scallops, small side muscles removed

Salt and black pepper, to taste

½ cup finely chopped fresh chives, for garnish

sherried pumpkin bisque with pink and green peppercorns

In a heavy-bottomed, 12-quart pot, cook the onion in the olive oil and butter over moderate heat 5 minutes. Add the green peppercorns, coriander, allspice, mace, cloves, and pumpkin and cook, stirring constantly, 7 minutes. Add the vegetable stock and cream and bring to a boil over high heat. Reduce the heat to moderate and simmer 20 minutes or until the pumpkin is very tender. Cool slightly.

In a blender, purée the mixture in batches until very smooth. Return to the pot and add the sherry, vinegar, and pink peppercorns. Bring to a boil over high heat, stirring frequently. Reduce the heat to moderate and cook 10 minutes. Season with salt and pepper. Serve immediately.

➤ When crisp, cool days bring cravings for a heartwarming and soothing vegetable soup, serve this velvety bisque. Its spicy, rich flavors will brighten even the dreariest day.

HOTTER 4

makes about 6 servings

1 large onion, coarsely chopped

2 tablespoons olive oil

2 tablespoons unsalted butter

2 tablespoons green peppercorns

1 tablespoon ground coriander

$1/2$ teaspoon *each* ground allspice and mace

$1/4$ teaspoon ground cloves

1 small eating pumpkin (about 3 pounds), stemmed, halved, peeled, seeded, and cut into small dice (about 6 cups diced)

8 cups homemade vegetable stock (page 13) or canned vegetable broth (preferably low-sodium)

2 cups whipping cream

1 cup dry sherry

$1 1/2$ tablespoons sherry vinegar

$2 1/2$ tablespoons pink peppercorns

Salt and pepper, to taste

Chinese Hot and Sour Soup

PEPPERY, SOUR, AND SLIGHTLY SWEET FLAVORS FORM THE BACKBONE OF THIS CLASSIC CHINESE SOUP.
YOU MAY INCREASE THE AMOUNT OF PEPPERCORNS IF YOU CRAVE EXTRA HEAT.

*To facilitate slicing the pork, wrap the meat tightly in plastic and place in the freezer for thirty minutes prior to cutting.
You can buy all of the ingredients in any Asian market and some well-stocked grocery or natural food stores.*

MAKES 8 TO 10 SERVINGS. ⌣ HOTTEST #7

¾ cup rice wine vinegar

2½ tablespoons cornstarch

8 dried Chinese black mushrooms

3 dried cloud ear mushrooms

10 cups homemade chicken stock or low-sodium
    chicken broth

3 tablespoons each finely ground white and
    black peppercorns

3 tablespoons soy sauce

1½ teaspoons Chinese-style hot chili paste

1½ tablespoons peanut oil

½ pound pork tenderloin, cut into slivers
    approximately 2 inches long and ⅛ inch wide

4 cloves garlic, minced

1⅓ cups julienned bamboo shoots

Two 5-ounce blocks firm tofu, cut into ¼-inch cubes

3 eggs, lightly beaten

Salt and additional black pepper, to taste

5 scallions, trimmed and cut on the diagonal into
    ½-inch pieces

In a small bowl, combine the vinegar and cornstarch; mix well. Set aside.

Soak the black and cloud ear mushrooms in warm water to cover for 10 to 15 minutes, or until soft and pliable. Drain well and discard the soaking liquid. Remove the stems and discard. Coarsely chop the black mushrooms, and cut the cloud ear mushrooms into long slivers approximately ⅛ inch wide. Place in a 6-quart, heavy-bottomed saucepan.

To the mushrooms add the chicken stock, ground pepper, soy sauce, and chili paste. Bring to a boil over high heat and cook 7 minutes, stirring occasionally. Reduce the heat to moderately low while you prepare the remaining ingredients.

In a large, nonstick sauté pan, heat the peanut oil over high heat until it just begins to smoke. Add the pork, garlic, and bamboo shoots and cook 30 seconds, stirring constantly. Add to the stock along with the vinegar-cornstarch mixture and tofu, and bring to a boil over high heat. Cook, stirring frequently, for 3 to 4 minutes, or until the soup is thick and aromatic.

Slowly add the eggs in a thin stream, stirring gently with a large fork to make long, delicate strands. Remove from the heat and season with salt and more pepper, if desired. Add the scallions just before serving.

chilled cream of asparagus soup with green peppercorns

1 1/2 **pounds asparagus, trimmed, stalks coarsely chopped, and tips reserved**

3 **shallots, coarsely chopped**

1 1/2 **tablespoons green peppercorns, finely ground**

2 **tablespoons vegetable or light olive oil**

5 **cups homemade vegetable stock (page 13) or canned vegetable broth (preferably low-sodium)**

1 1/2 **cups whipping cream**

Salt and pepper, to taste

1/3 **cup finely chopped fresh chives, for garnish (optional)**

➤ Pair this silky soup with a salad of mixed greens for a delightful spring or summer lunch. Combined with a composed salad of assorted spring vegetables and warm rolls, the soup becomes a complete dinner.

HOT 2

makes 4 to 6 servings

In a 3-quart, heavy-bottomed saucepan, sauté the asparagus stalks (not the tips), shallots, and peppercorns in the vegetable oil over moderately high heat 3 to 5 minutes, stirring occasionally. Add the vegetable stock and cream and bring to a boil over high heat, stirring frequently to prevent the mixture from boiling over. Reduce the heat to moderate and cook 8 to 10 minutes, or until asparagus is tender but not mushy. Remove from the heat and cool slightly.

Using a blender, purée the mixture in batches until smooth. Strain through a fine wire mesh or sieve and return to the saucepan. Bring to a boil over high heat, stirring frequently. Add the reserved asparagus tips and cook 1 minute, or until bright green and crisp-tender. Season with salt and pepper and remove from the heat.

Store in a tightly sealed container in the refrigerator until thoroughly chilled, about 4 hours. Serve cold, garnished with the chives, if desired.

two-peppercorn broccoli timbales

Preheat oven to 325° F. Lightly grease a six-cup jumbo muffin tin.

In a large bowl, beat the eggs until well mixed. Add the cream, cheeses, peppercorns, thyme, salt, nutmeg, and broccoli; mix well. Evenly distribute the broccoli and peppercorns among the six muffin cups. Pour the egg mixture over the broccoli.

Set the muffin tin in a 9-x-13-inch baking pan. Fill the baking pan with very hot water until it reaches just over halfway up the sides of the muffin tin. Bake in the center of the oven 45 to 50 minutes, or until a toothpick inserted into the centers comes out clean. Remove from the oven and let stand at room temperature for 10 minutes before unmolding.

To unmold: Hold a baking sheet tightly over the muffin pan. With one quick motion, flip both pans over together, so that the timbales gently fall onto the baking sheet. Place the baking sheet on a flat surface and gently lift the muffin pan. Arrange on plates and serve immediately.

➤ For the consummate special-occasion meal, present these individual vegetable custards surrounded by angel hair pasta that has been anointed with good olive oil and laced with fresh herbs.

I use a jumbo muffin pan composed of six $^2/_3$-cup capacity muffin cups for this elegant dish.

HOT 3

makes 4 servings

4 eggs

2 cups heavy cream, warmed

2 ounces Parmesan cheese, finely grated

2 ounces Monterey Jack cheese, finely grated

1$^1/_2$ tablespoons coarsely ground white peppercorns

1$^1/_2$ tablespoons pink peppercorns

2 teaspoons dried thyme

1 teaspoon kosher or sea salt

$^1/_2$ teaspoon ground nutmeg

3$^1/_2$ cups small broccoli flowerettes, blanched

peppered summer squash frittata

3 small zucchini, cut into ¼-inch cubes

2 small yellow crookneck squash, cut into ¼-inch cubes

2 small pattypan squash, cut into ¼-inch cubes

1 small onion, finely diced

2 tablespoons peanut or vegetable oil

12 large eggs

2 teaspoons *each* white and black peppercorns, coarsely ground

1 teaspoon pink peppercorns

1½ tablespoons minced fresh thyme

Fresh herb sprigs, for garnish

➤ Simple to make and easy to transport, this versatile summer-vegetable frittata is a great do-ahead dish for everything from small get-togethers to large picnics. Accompany with imported olives, assorted cheeses, and crackers and bread.

The recipe can easily be doubled and baked in two 10-inch sauté pans.

HOTTER 4

makes about 6 servings

Preheat oven to 325° F.

In a large sauté pan, cook the squash and onion in the oil over high heat, stirring frequently, 3 to 4 minutes or until crisp-tender. Transfer to a large bowl and cool to room temperature. When cool, add the eggs, peppercorns, and thyme. Mix well.

Place a nonstick ovenproof 10-inch sauté pan (with sloped sides) over moderately high heat. When the pan is warm, add the egg mixture and stir quickly from the outside of the pan toward the center (as if making scrambled eggs), until about one quarter of the mixture is set. Smooth the top, remove from the heat, and transfer to the middle rack of the oven. Bake 25 to 30 minutes, or until the center is set. Do not overbake the frittata. Remove from the oven and cool to room temperature.

To unmold, run a dull knife around the outside edges of the pan, gently pulling the frittata up and toward the center to loosen it from the bottom of the pan. Firmly hold a platter over the top of the pan and, with one quick movement, flip the pan and the platter over together, so that the frittata gently unmolds onto the platter. Serve at room temperature, sliced into wedges and garnished with herb sprigs.

winter root vegetable gratin with peppercorns

Preheat oven to 400° F. Generously grease a 9-x-12-inch baking pan.

In a very large bowl, combine the cream, peppercorns, nutmeg, and orange zest. Set aside.

Bring 4 quarts of salted water to boil in a large pot. Add the parsnips, turnips, and rutabaga and cook 2 minutes. Drain immediately in a colander and add to the cream; toss gently. Transfer to the prepared pan and place on the middle rack of the oven. Bake 30 minutes. Remove from the oven and evenly sprinkle the bread crumbs over the top. Return to the oven and bake 25 to 30 minutes, or until the top is brown and the vegetables are tender. Remove from the oven and let stand at room temperature 5 to 7 minutes before cutting into squares or rectangles. Garnish with the parsley.

➤ In cool-weather months, nothing satisfies like these earthy root vegetables cloaked in a rich, peppercorn-accented cream sauce. For a substantial lunch or light supper, pair with a salad of mixed greens tossed with apples and garnished with toasted walnuts.

HOT 2

makes 6 to 8 servings

3 1/2 cups whipping cream

1 tablespoon finely ground black peppercorns

1 1/2 teaspoons coarsely ground white peppercorns

1 teaspoon finely ground green peppercorns

1/2 teaspoon ground nutmeg

1 tablespoon finely minced orange zest

4 medium parsnips, trimmed and thinly sliced on the diagonal

2 small turnips, trimmed, halved, and thinly sliced

1 medium rutabaga, trimmed, halved, and thinly sliced

1 cup finely ground dried bread crumbs

1/3 cup minced fresh parsley, for garnish

Broccoli and Red Bell Pepper Salad with Black and White Peppercorns

SERVE THIS COLORFUL, ROOM TEMPERATURE SALAD AS A SIDE DISH OR ACCOMPANIED
WITH BREAD STICKS FOR A LIGHT, HEALTHFUL LUNCH.

When exposed to vinegar (or other acids) for more than twenty or thirty minutes, green vegetables take on an unpleasant gray tone, losing their crunchy texture and vivid color. For this reason, if you plan to hold this salad longer than twenty minutes before serving, either omit the vinegar when making the vinaigrette and sprinkle the dressed vegetables with the vinegar just before serving, or prepare the vegetables and the vinaigrette separately and combine the two just before serving.

MAKES ABOUT 6 SERVINGS. ∼ **HOTTER #4**

In an 8-quart saucepan, bring 4 quarts of salted water to boil over high heat. Have ready a large bowl filled with ice water. Drop the broccoli into the boiling water and stir well. Cook 30 to 45 seconds or until the broccoli is crisp-tender and bright green. Drain in a colander and refresh with cold water. Immediately plunge into the ice water and swish around using your hands. When the broccoli is thoroughly chilled, drain well in a colander. Lay the broccoli in a single layer on clean kitchen towels and pat dry. Place in a large bowl along with the red bell pepper.

In a small bowl, combine the olive oil and peppercorns. Slowly add the vinegar, whisking constantly with a wire whisk to form a smooth emulsion. Add the garlic and salt and mix well. Add to the vegetables and toss gently. Adjust the seasoning and sprinkle with pine nuts. Serve immediately.

8 cups broccoli florets (about 2 large heads)

1 large red bell pepper, stemmed, seeded, and julienned

½ cup olive oil

1½ teaspoons each finely ground white and black peppercorns

1 tablespoon each slightly crushed white and black peppercorns

2 tablespoons balsamic vinegar

2 cloves garlic, minced

Salt, to taste

½ cup toasted pine nuts

Lobster-Grapefruit Salad with Pink Peppercorns

Ultimately elegant and refined, this special occasion salad is ideal for a light warm-weather supper, served with champagne or a crisp sauvignon blanc. If you can't find lobster tails, use jumbo prawns instead.
Makes 4 to 6 servings.   Hot: rated 2

Using kitchen scissors or a very sharp knife, remove the lobster meat from the shells. Save the shells for making stock or discard. Place the lobster meat and the wine in a shallow saucepan. Bring to a boil over high heat, reduce the heat to moderate, and cook for 2 to 3 minutes or until the lobster is just done. Do not overcook the lobster meat. Remove with a slotted spoon and cool to room temperature, reserving the wine.

When the meat is cool enough to handle, slice it into ½-inch rounds and arrange around the inner edge of a large plate. Arrange the grapefruit fillets between the slices of lobster.

To make the vinaigrette: Place the shallots in the reserved wine and bring to a boil over high heat. Boil until liquid is reduced to 2 tablespoons. Place in a large bowl and cool to room temperature. Using a wire whisk, incorporate small amounts of the olive oil, whisking all the while. Slowly add the grapefruit juice and vinegar, whisking all the while to form a smooth emulsion. Add the peppercorns; mix well and season with salt.

Place the endive in a bowl and dress with half of the vinaigrette; mix gently. Arrange endive in a mound in the center of the lobster and grapefruit. Drizzle the lobster and grapefruit with the remaining vinaigrette, and serve at room temperature.

Note: To cut citrus fruit into fillets, use a very sharp paring knife to first peel the fruit, taking care to remove all the pith. Then cut between the fibers that separate each section in order to remove the pulp, leaving behind the white membrane. Gently lay each fillet on a flat surface as you remove it from the whole fruit.

4 lobster tails (about 1 pound each in the shell)

1 cup white wine

2 large pink grapefruits, cut into fillets (see Note)

Vinaigrette:

2 shallots, peeled and thinly sliced

1 cup olive oil

2 tablespoons grapefruit juice

2 tablespoons champagne vinegar

2½ tablespoons red peppercorns, bruised

Salt, to taste

2 firm heads endive, trimmed and slivered

Mussels and Prawns with
Orange-Pink Peppercorn Vinaigrette

This warm salad of fresh mussels and prawns is elegant and light, and at its best when served with a toasty champagne or a buttery chardonnay. You might serve the seafood on a bed of rocket or baby greens as well as with angel hair pasta. Makes 4 servings. *Hot: rated 2*

Bring a large pot of water to boil over high heat. When the water is boiling, add the prawns and cook for 1 minute. Drain and rinse with cold water. When the prawns are cool enough to handle, remove the shells and tails. Place in a bowl.

Scrub the shells of the mussels and remove the beards. Place the mussels and the wine in a shallow skillet. Bring to a boil over high heat, cover, reduce the heat to moderate, and cook for 4 to 5 minutes, or until all the shells have opened. Remove all those that have opened, and cook the remaining mussels in the wine for 2 minutes. Discard any that have not opened. When the opened shells are cool enough to handle, remove the mussels and add to the prawns.

To make the vinaigrette: place the orange juice, saffron, and peppercorns in a small saucepan. Over moderate heat, stir constantly until the orange juice is hot and the saffron is soft, 4 to 5 minutes. Remove from the heat and cool to room temperature.

Place the walnut oil and garlic in a bowl. Slowly add the champagne vinegar, whisking all the while to form a smooth emulsion. Add the orange juice mixture slowly, whisking all the while. Season with salt and pepper.

Add the vinaigrette to the seafood and mix gently. Arrange around the buttered pasta, or on top of greens, and garnish with the chives.

½ pound medium-sized prawns

12-15 mussels (make sure the shells are closed when you buy them)

1 cup dry white wine

Vinaigrette:

3 tablespoons orange juice

1 teaspoon saffron

3 tablespoons pink peppercorns

¾ cup walnut oil

1 clove garlic, minced

2 tablespoons champagne vinegar

Salt and pepper, to taste

½ cup chopped fresh chives, for garnish

Chive blossoms (optional), for garnish

Peppery Chicken-Fried Rice

A LIVELY MIXTURE OF COARSELY GROUND AND WHOLE PEPPERCORNS GIVES THIS CLASSIC CHINESE DISH A DEFINITE KICK.
TO FACILITATE CUTTING THE CHICKEN INTO SMALL PIECES, WRAP THE BONED AND SKINNED BREASTS IN PLASTIC AND FREEZE FOR
THIRTY MINUTES PRIOR TO DICING. YOU MAY SUBSTITUTE DICED SMOKED HAM FOR THE CHICKEN IF YOU WISH.

MAKES ABOUT 6 SERVINGS. ‿ **HOTTEST #7**

Bring 4 quarts of salted water to boil in an 8-quart pot. Add the rice, stir well, and return to a boil. Cook 10 minutes, or until the rice is just tender. Take care not to overcook the rice. Drain in a colander and refresh with cold water. Spread the rice in a thin layer on a baking sheet and refrigerate until cold. Alternatively, cover with plastic or foil and refrigerate overnight.

In a very large nonstick sauté pan or wok, heat the oil over high heat until it just begins to smoke. Add the chicken, bell pepper, ginger, scallions, garlic, and peppercorns and cook 1 minute, stirring constantly. Add the green peas, cooked rice, soy sauce, and vinegar and cook 1 minute, stirring constantly.

Make a large well in the center of the rice mixture, clearing a space in the pan. Add the eggs and cook, stirring frequently, until they just begin to set—like scrambled eggs. Immediately remove the pan from the heat. Using a fork, stir the eggs into the rice mixture. Serve immediately with additional soy sauce on the side, if desired.

1½ cups long-grain white rice

¼ cup peanut oil

2 boneless, skinless chicken breast halves, cut into ¼-inch cubes

1 red or yellow bell pepper, stemmed, seeded, and cut into small dice

2-inch piece fresh ginger root, peeled and finely chopped

6 scallions, trimmed and finely chopped

3 cloves garlic, finely chopped

1 tablespoon each coarsely ground black and white peppercorns

2 teaspoons each whole pink and green peppercorns

1 cup cooked English green peas

2½ tablespoons light soy sauce

1½ tablespoons rice wine vinegar

6 eggs, well beaten

Vietnamese Salt and Pepper Prawns

1 pound jumbo prawns

2 tablespoons each coarsely ground black and Szechuan peppercorns

2 tablespoons Kosher or other coarse salt

1 tablespoon sugar

4 cloves garlic, minced

¼ cup homemade beef stock or unsalted beef broth

3 tablespoons *nuoc cham* (fish sauce)

3 tablespoons fresh lime juice

Traditionally, these prawns are served in the shell as they are described here in this recipe. The action of the salt and pepper (along with the liquid flavoring ingredients) serves as a tenderizer and reduces cooking time considerably. Cooking in the shell is best, but if you simply can't stand to peel your own shrimp at the table, remove the shells first (leaving the tails intact) and proceed with the recipe. Serve this simple seafood dish with stir-fried vegetables, noodles or rice, and perhaps a Vietnamese beef or vegetable salad.
Makes 4 servings.   Hot: rated 3

Combine all the ingredients in a nonreactive bowl and mix well. Let stand at room temperature for 1 hour, or in the refrigerator for up to 24 hours.

Preheat oven to 450° F.

Transfer the prawns and the marinade to a baking pan. Bake for 5 minutes. Remove from oven and serve prawns immediately.

Pasta with Peppered Artichokes, Ham, and Toasted Almonds

THIS PASTA DISH COMBINES SOME OF MY FAVORITE INGREDIENTS. I PREFER USING FRESH BABY ARTICHOKES, BUT IF YOU ARE PRESSED FOR TIME, OR IF YOU CANNOT FIND THE FRESH VERSION, SUBSTITUTE PRECOOKED, MARINATED ARTICHOKE HEARTS SOLD IN JARS. STRAIN THE CHOKES BEFORE USING THEM IN THE PASTA, BUT SAVE THE MARINATING LIQUID TO USE IN OTHER DISHES.

MAKES 6 TO 8 SERVINGS. ⌒ **HOT #3**

1 large onion, cut into medium dice

4 cloves garlic, finely chopped

⅔ cup olive oil

1 tablespoon finely ground white peppercorns

2 teaspoons drained whole green peppercorns packed in brine

1 teaspoon dried thyme

1 cup dry white wine

1½ cups cooked baby artichoke hearts, quartered

Two ½-inch slices smoked ham (about 1 pound), cut into ½-inch cubes

1 pound medium-sized pasta shells

⅓ pound imported Parmesan cheese, finely grated

½ cup coarsely chopped toasted almonds

Salt and black pepper, to taste

In a very large, nonstick sauté pan, cook the onion and garlic in 3 tablespoons of the olive oil over moderately high heat for 7 minutes, stirring frequently. Add the peppercorns, thyme, and wine and cook 5 minutes, stirring occasionally. Add the artichoke hearts and ham and mix gently. Remove from the heat and set aside until needed.

In a 10-quart pot, bring 7 quarts of salted water to a boil over high heat. Add the pasta and stir well. Return to a boil and cook 12 to 13 minutes, or until the pasta is al dente. Drain well in a colander and immediately place in a very large bowl. Add the remaining olive oil and toss well.

Reheat the vegetable-ham mixture over high heat, stirring constantly, just until heated through, about 1½ minutes. Add to the pasta along with half of the grated cheese and the almonds. Season with salt and pepper and toss gently. Serve immediately, and pass the remaining cheese on the side.

Seared Four-Peppercorn Swordfish with Coriander

ASK YOUR FISHMONGER TO SLICE EXTRA-THICK STEAKS FROM THE WHOLE FISH WHEN PURCHASING THE
SWORDFISH FOR THIS RECIPE. SERVED HOT OR CHILLED, THESE PEPPERCORN- AND CORIANDER-ENCRUSTED STEAKS ARE
TERRIFIC SERVED WITH HOMEMADE AIOLI OR SIMPLY DRIZZLED WITH FRESH LEMON JUICE.

MAKES 4 SERVINGS. ∿ **HOTTER #5**

In a small bowl, combine the peppercorns, salt, coriander, and 3 tablespoons of the olive oil; mix well. Pat the mixture on both sides of each swordfish steak, slightly pressing the peppercorns and coriander into the fish. Let stand at room temperature for 15 minutes.

In a large, nonstick sauté pan, heat the remaining 2 tablespoons olive oil over moderately high heat. When the oil is hot but not smoking, add the fish steaks and cook 2 minutes on the first side. Gently flip the steaks over and cook second side 2 to 3 minutes, or until the steaks are cooked on the exterior but still pink in the center. Remove the fish from the pan and transfer to a large platter or individual plates. Serve immediately, garnished with lemon wedges.

2 tablespoons each coarsely ground black and white peppercorns

1 tablespoon each coarsely ground pink and green peppercorns

1 tablespoon kosher or sea salt

2 rounded teaspoons ground coriander

5 tablespoons olive oil

Four 1-inch-thick swordfish steaks (about 8 ounces each), patted dry

Lemon wedges, for garnish

Mediterranean Seafood Stew with Fennel and Peppercorns

DON'T BE INTIMIDATED BY THE LONG LIST OF INGREDIENTS, MANY OF WHICH ARE HERBS AND PEPPERCORNS THAT REQUIRE NO PREPARATION. THIS ZIPPY SEAFOOD STEW TAKES LESS THAN ONE HOUR TO MAKE, AND WHEN COUPLED WITH HOT BREAD AND A SALAD, MAKES A WONDERFULLY INVITING DISH FOR COMPANY.

When buying the fresh mussels and clams, be sure to purchase only those with closed shells.
MAKES 6 TO 8 SERVINGS. ∼ **HOTTER #6**

4 cloves garlic, thinly sliced

2 large bulbs fennel, trimmed, halved, cored, and cut into ½-inch dice

1 tablespoon drained whole green peppercorns packed in brine

1 tablespoon coarsely ground black peppercorns

2 teaspoons each slightly crushed white and pink peppercorns

¼ cup olive oil

½ teaspoon each dried rosemary, thyme, and oregano

3 medium tomatoes, cored and finely diced

1 cup dry white wine

1½ pounds fresh mussels (about 20 to 22), beards removed and shells scrubbed

1 pound Manila or any other small fresh clams (about 18 to 20), shells scrubbed

4 cups clam juice or strong fish stock

8 small new potatoes, cut into eighths

¾ pound medium prawns, peeled and tails removed

¾ pound scallops, small side muscles removed

Salt and additional black pepper, to taste

½ cup finely chopped fresh parsley, for garnish

In a large, heavy-bottomed saucepan, cook the garlic, fennel, and peppercorns in the olive oil over moderate heat for 7 to 8 minutes, stirring frequently. Add the herbs, tomatoes, and wine and bring to a boil over high heat; cook 3 minutes, stirring frequently. Add the mussels and clams, cover with a tight-fitting lid, and cook 3 or 4 minutes, stirring once or twice. Remove the lid and, using kitchen tongs, remove all mussels and clams with opened shells; place in a bowl and set aside. Return the lid to the pot and cook an additional minute; remove all mussels and clams with opened shells and add to the others. Discard any with closed shells.

Add the clam juice and potatoes to the pot. Return to the boil and cook 12 to 15 minutes, or until the potatoes are tender. Meanwhile, remove the mussels and clams from their shells, place in a small bowl, and set aside. Discard the shells.

Add the prawns and scallops to the stew and cook 1½ minutes, stirring frequently. Add the reserved mussels and clams and cook 30 seconds, or just until the prawns and scallops are cooked through and the shellfish is hot. Take care not to overcook the seafood. Season with salt and more pepper, if desired. Serve immediately, garnished with the parsley.

Four-Peppercorn Filet Mignon

For a classic French bistro supper serve this peppery filet with French-fried potatoes. Baked or pan-fried potatoes are also a good complement, and a green salad or broccoli makes this a simple, balanced dinner.
Makes 4 servings.   *Hotter: rated 4*

Combine the peppercorns, salt, and olive oil in a shallow dish; mix well. Coat each piece of meat with this mixture, taking care to coat both sides equally.

Set a nonstick skillet that is just large enough to accommodate the steaks over high heat. When the skillet is hot, add the steaks. Reduce the heat to moderately high and cook on the first side for 2 to 3 minutes. Carefully flip the steaks and continue cooking on the other side. The total cooking time depends on how you like your meat cooked. I suggest medium rare.

Remove the steaks to a large platter and keep warm in a low oven while you prepare the sauce. Remove the leftover peppercorns and oil from the skillet and return it to the heat.

Add the garlic and brandy to the skillet and cook over high heat for 1 minute. Add the cream and cook over high heat, stirring all the while, until it is thick enough to coat the back of a spoon, 3 to 4 minutes. Drizzle the sauce over the meat and serve immediately.

2 tablespoons each pink, green, white, and black peppercorns, lightly crushed

2 teaspoons Kosher or other coarse salt

2 tablespoons olive oil

4 8-ounce filet mignon steaks, trimmed of excess fat

6 cloves garlic, minced

½ cup brandy or cognac

1 cup heavy cream

Chinese Braised Short Ribs with Black Pepper

These ultratender beef ribs are at once peppery and slightly sweet. Served with stir-fried green vegetables and steamed rice, these ribs make an unforgettable meal for those who enjoy the intense flavors of Chinese cuisine.
Makes 4 servings.   *Hotter: rated 5*

In a deep-sided pan, cook the ribs in the peanut oil over high heat until they are browned on all sides. Add the garlic, ginger, peppercorns, and anise, and cook for 1 minute. Add the red wine and continue cooking until it evaporates. Add the beef stock, soy sauce, oyster sauce, vinegar, and brown sugar and bring to a boil.

Reduce the heat to moderately low; cover and cook for 1 hour or until the meat is very tender and the sauce is thick and aromatic. Using a spoon, remove the excess fat from the sauce. Add all but 2 tablespoons of the green onions; mix gently. Garnish with the remaining green onions, and with the star anise and kumquats if desired.

2 pounds English short ribs, cut in 2-inch lengths

2 tablespoons peanut oil

4 cloves garlic, thinly sliced

1-inch piece ginger root, peeled and minced

2 tablespoons each coarsely ground black and Szechuan peppercorns

3 star anise (more for garnish, if desired)

1 cup dry red wine

2 cups homemade beef stock or unsalted beef broth

¼ cup soy sauce

3 tablespoons oyster sauce

3 tablespoons Chinese black vinegar

2 tablespoons brown sugar

1 small bunch green onions, trimmed and minced (reserve some for garnish)

Kumquats, for garnish (optional)

Braised Duck with Green Peppercorns and Prunes

1 pound bacon

1 pound small boiling onions, trimmed and peeled (see Note)

6 duck legs (about 4 pounds)

1 cup all-purpose flour

2 teaspoons each dried thyme, rosemary, and sage

1 cup dry sherry

2 quarts chicken stock (preferably homemade)

1⅓ cups pitted prunes, coarsely chopped

¼ cup coarsely ground green peppercorns

¼ cup whole green peppercorns in brine, drained

Salt and pepper, to taste

¾ cup chopped parsley, for garnish

Slightly sweet and piquant, this French-inspired duck stew is rich and robust. It's terrific served with grilled or soft polenta, wild rice, or pasta. To save time, you may use frozen pearl onions rather than fresh.
Makes 4 to 6 servings.   *Hot: rated 3*

In a very large sauté pan, cook the bacon until almost crisp. Remove with a slotted spoon, reserving the fat, and drain on paper towels. When cool, coarsely chop and place in a large bowl.

Cook the onions in the bacon fat over moderate heat for 8 to 10 minutes, stirring from time to time, until they are golden brown on all sides. Remove with a slotted spoon and add to the bacon. Transfer ¼ cup of the fat to a deep, heavy-bottomed saucepan. Discard the remaining fat.

Dredge the duck legs in the flour, making sure they are coated on all sides. Heat the bacon fat. When the fat is hot, add the duck legs and brown on all sides over moderate heat. Add the herbs and sherry and cook over high heat until the liquid almost evaporates, 4 to 5 minutes. Add 6 cups of the chicken stock and bring to a boil. Reduce the heat to moderate and cook until the duck is very tender and the liquid has almost evaporated, about 1½ hours.

Using a slotted spoon, remove the duck legs from the liquid and place in a colander. When cool enough to handle, remove the meat from the bones, taking care to remove the skin, tendons, and fat from the meat.

Add the chunks of meat to the bacon and onions, along with the prunes and peppercorns. Return to the cooking liquid along with the remaining 2 cups of chicken stock. Bring to a boil over high heat, reduce the heat to moderate, and cook for 25 to 30 minutes or until the liquid is slightly thickened and the stew is hot. Season with salt and pepper and garnish with the chopped parsley.

Note: To loosen the skin of fresh pearl onions, blanch in boiling water for 1 minute; drain, and cool slightly. Use a paring knife to remove the skin and trim the stem ends.

Poached Chicken Breasts with Peppercorn Sauce

COOL IN TEMPERATURE YET WARM IN FLAVOR, THIS ELEGANT CHICKEN DISH GOES WELL WITH A GREEN SALAD,
FRESH CORN, OR STEAMED ASPARAGUS FOR A PLEASING HOT-WEATHER SUPPER.

MAKES 4 SERVINGS. ∾ HOTTER #5

In a shallow saucepan, place the chicken, wine, water, and pepper-corns. (The chicken should be completely submerged in liquid, so add additional water and/or wine to cover, if necessary.) Bring to a boil over high heat. Reduce the heat to moderately low, cover tightly, and simmer 10 to 12 minutes, or until the chicken is just cooked through. Remove the chicken with a slotted spoon, reserving the liquid, and drain in a colander. Cool chicken to room temperature. When cool, keeping the breast meat intact, remove and discard the skin, bones, cartilage, and tendons. Cover the chicken breasts with a damp kitchen towel and set aside.

To make the sauce, cook the reserved poaching liquid over high heat, stirring frequently, for 30 to 35 minutes, or until reduced to about ⅓ cup. Transfer to a medium bowl and cool to room temperature. When cool, add the mayonnaise and season with salt and more pepper, if desired. Serve the chicken breasts slightly chilled or at room temperature, topped with the sauce and garnished with the parsley.

4 large chicken breast halves

3 cups dry white wine

3 cups water

1½ teaspoons coarsely ground black peppercorns

1½ teaspoons whole pink peppercorns

1 teaspoon drained whole green peppercorns packed in brine

½ cup mayonnaise, preferably homemade

Salt and additional black pepper, to taste

Sprigs of parsley, for garnish

three-pepper corn muffins

1 1/2 cups fine yellow cornmeal

1 cup unbleached or all-purpose flour

1/2 cup sugar

1 tablespoon *each* black and white peppercorns, coarsely ground

2 teaspoons green peppercorns

1 teaspoon kosher salt

1 1/4 cups buttermilk

3 large eggs

12 tablespoons (1 1/2 sticks) unsalted butter, melted and cooled slightly

1/3 pound sharp Cheddar cheese, finely grated

➤ Even my mom, who isn't a fan of corn bread, found these plump corn muffins, enriched with Cheddar cheese and spiked with peppercorns, tempting and delicious.

Serve with red beans and rice, black-eyed peas, or meatless Louisiana-style gumbo. These muffins are also good spread with softened cream cheese and topped with fresh tomato slices.

HOT 3

makes 12 standard muffins or 6 jumbo muffins

Preheat oven to 350° F. Generously grease two standard muffin tins (12 cups) or one jumbo muffin tin (6 cups).

In a large bowl, combine the cornmeal, flour, sugar, peppercorns, and salt. Mix well and set aside.

In a medium bowl, combine the buttermilk and eggs, whisking well to thoroughly combine. Add the butter and cheese and mix well.

Make a well in the center of the dry ingredients. Slowly add the wet ingredients, mixing with a large fork until *just combined*. Do not overmix the batter. Using a large spoon, fill each muffin cup three-quarters full with batter. Place the pan(s) on the bottom rack of the oven and bake 10 minutes, rotating the pan(s) once from front to back. Place pan(s) on top rack and bake an additional 7 or 8 minutes, or until a toothpick inserted in the center of a muffin comes out clean and the tops are barely light golden brown. Do not overbake the muffins.

Remove from the oven and let stand 5 to 7 minutes. Gently remove muffins from pans and cool on racks. Serve warm or at room temperature. Muffins may be stored tightly wrapped in foil at room temperature for 1 or 2 days.

Four-Peppercorn Spice Butter

Use this flavorful, slightly sweet butter for vegetables; to melt on top of grilled or broiled fish, poultry, or meat; or to toss with hot pasta as a simple sauce. Mixed with garlic, this butter would make an intriguing peppery spread for toast.
Makes ¼ pound seasoned butter.   Hot: rated 2

Combine the above ingredients in a small bowl; mix well. You may store the butter in a covered container in the refrigerator for up to 1 week. Alternately, form it into a cylinder, wrap in wax or parchment paper, and freeze; slice rounds as needed.

¼ pound (1 stick) unsalted butter, softened

2 teaspoons coarsely ground allspice

1½ teaspoons each ground green, pink, white, black peppercorns

½ teaspoon salt

Port-Poached Dried Fruits
with Black Pepper

This dish is ideal for fall or winter desserts, or for a heartwarming breakfast or brunch. The spicy compote is also good with roasted pork or lamb or with ice cream, accompanied by chunks of bittersweet chocolate or a simple butter or chocolate cake, or drizzled with crème fraîche.
Makes about 6 servings.   *Hot: rated 3*

Place the port, water, sugar, and peppercorns in a heavy-bottomed saucepan. Bring to a boil over high heat, stirring frequently; boil for 20 minutes or until the liquid begins to thicken and become syrupy. Add all the fruit, reduce the heat to moderate, cover, and cook for 15 to 20 minutes or until the fruit is tender but not mushy.

Add the vanilla; mix well and serve warm or at room temperature in shallow bowls. Garnish with a sprig of mint.

1 bottle (750 ml) port

2 cups water

1 cup sugar

¼ cup black peppercorns

1 cup dried figs, stemmed and halved

1 cup dried apricots

½ cup pitted prunes

½ cup dried apple rings, halved (or quartered if large)

½ cup dried pineapple rings, quartered

½ cup dried cherries or cranberries

3 tablespoons vanilla extract

Mint sprigs, for garnish

Vanilla Rice Pudding with Green and Pink Peppercorns

HEADY WITH THE ESSENCE OF VANILLA, EACH BITE OF THIS DESSERT DELIVERS A SURPRISE PUNCH PROVIDED BY
PINK AND GREEN PEPPERCORNS. PRESENTED WARM IN THE COOLER MONTHS OR CHILLED DURING SUMMERTIME,
THIS UNIQUE RICE PUDDING IS SURE TO STIMULATE TASTE BUDS ANY TIME OF YEAR!

MAKES 6 TO 8 SERVINGS. ⁓ **HOT #3**

4 cups half-and-half

1 teaspoon finely ground pink peppercorns

½ teaspoon each whole pink and green peppercorns

½ teaspoon finely ground black peppercorns

1 vanilla pod, split lengthwise and beans removed

¾ cup short-grained white rice, such as arborio

¾ cup sugar

Pinch salt

½ teaspoon each ground cinnamon and nutmeg

2 cups whole milk

Juice from 1 large orange

Zest from 1 lemon

2 teaspoons vanilla extract

In a 6-quart saucepan, place the half-and-half, peppercorns, and vanilla beans. Bring to a boil over high heat, stirring constantly to prevent the liquid from boiling over. Reduce the heat to moderate and simmer, stirring frequently, for 10 minutes.

Add the rice, sugar, salt, cinnamon, and nutmeg and bring to a boil over high heat. Reduce the heat to moderate and cook 15 minutes, stirring frequently. Add the milk and cook about 40 minutes, stirring occasionally, until the rice is very tender and the mixture is thick and creamy.

Add the orange juice, lemon zest, and vanilla extract; mix well and cook 2 minutes. Remove from the heat. Serve immediately or cool to room temperature, transfer to a storage container, and cover the surface with plastic wrap. Refrigerate until thoroughly chilled.

Chocolate-Hazelnut Mousse with Black Pepper

MEDIUM-GROUND BLACK PEPPERCORNS LEND A DEEP, WARM ACCENT TO THIS RICH, HAZELNUT-SCENTED CHOCOLATE MOUSSE. SERVE WITH FRANGELICO OR ESPRESSO FOR A MEMORABLE DESSERT.

If you cannot find superfine sugar (super-granulated white sugar) in the grocery store, make your own by placing regular granulated sugar in a food processor or blender and processing until fine, five to seven minutes. Do not overprocess the sugar or it will turn to powder.

MAKES ABOUT 6 SERVINGS. ∼ HOT #2

10 ounces high-quality bittersweet chocolate, coarsely chopped

2 cups heavy cream

3 tablespoons superfine sugar

2 tablespoons Frangelico liqueur (or any hazelnut-flavored liqueur)

1 tablespoon medium-ground black peppercorns

2 extra-large egg whites

½ cup finely chopped toasted hazelnuts, for garnish

In the top of a double boiler set over simmering water, combine the chocolate, ½ cup of the heavy cream, and the sugar, Frangelico, and black pepper. Cook for 2 to 3 minutes, stirring constantly, until the chocolate is completely melted and the mixture is smooth. Remove from the heat and cool to room temperature.

In a small, chilled bowl, whip the remaining 1½ cups heavy cream until stiff peaks form. Refrigerate until needed.

In a small bowl, whip the egg whites until soft peaks form. Gently fold the egg whites into the cooled chocolate mixture until just combined. Gently fold in the whipped cream until thoroughly blended. Do not overmix or the mousse will have an unpleasant texture. Cover with plastic or foil and refrigerate for at least 4 hours, or up to 2 days. Remove the mousse from the refrigerator 30 minutes before serving. Stir well and spoon into attractive glasses or small bowls and garnish with the hazelnuts.

Figs with White Peppercorn Syrup and Basil

½ cup white peppercorns, bruised

1 large bunch fresh basil (stems included), coarsely chopped

3 cups water

1 cup white wine

2 cups sugar

2 cups dried black figs, stemmed

2 tablespoons whole white peppercorns, for garnish

6 sprigs basil or mint, for garnish

Lavender, or other edible flowers, for garnish

The recipe calls for dried figs, but if fresh are in season feel free to use them instead. If serving fresh figs, make the syrup according to the recipe, but add the fresh figs to the finished syrup just before serving. This sweet-peppery dessert is delicious and light on its own, and richer served with ice cream or pound cake. Makes 4 to 6 servings. Hotter: rated 6

Place the bruised peppercorns, basil, water, and wine in a heavy-bottomed saucepan. Bring to a boil over high heat, and continue boiling for 10 minutes. Add the sugar and return to a boil. Cook over high heat for 15 to 20 minutes, or until the liquid is thick and syrupy. Strain through a fine wire mesh and return to the saucepan.

Add the figs to the syrup and cook over moderate heat for 10 to 15 minutes or until the figs are very tender. Serve warm with some of the syrup and garnish with the whole peppercorns, sprigs of basil or mint, and optionally with edible flowers.

strawberry-blackberry sorbet with pink and black peppercorns

1/4 cup fresh lemon juice

2 tablespoons blackberry (or other berry-flavored) liqueur

1 envelope unflavored gelatin

1/2 cup water

1 pint strawberries, stemmed and coarsely chopped

1 pint blackberries

3/4 to 1 cup sugar (depending on the sweetness of the berries)

1 tablespoon pink peppercorns, slightly crushed

1/2 teaspoon finely ground black peppercorns

Fresh mint sprigs, for garnish

➤ Ruby red and saturated with the flavor essence of berries, this peppercorn-flecked iced confection will thrill the taste buds and delight the eye. Serve as a palate refresher between courses, or with thin butter cookies for a summertime dessert.

HOT 3

makes 4 to 6 servings

Place the lemon juice and blackberry liqueur in a large bowl and mix well. Sprinkle the gelatin over the lemon juice mixture. Heat the water in a small saucepan until hot but not boiling. Add the water to the lemon juice–gelatin mixture, and mix well until gelatin is thoroughly dissolved.

To the gelatin mixture add the berries, sugar, and peppercorns; mix well. Using a blender, purée in batches until smooth. Strain through a fine wire mesh or sieve two times, or until no seeds remain. Transfer to a plastic container with a tight-fitting lid and place in the freezer for at least 6 hours. If you prefer an ultra-smooth texture, stir the mixture approximately once an hour during the first three hours of freezing.

To serve, remove from the freezer about 5 minutes before serving. When softened slightly, scoop into small balls using a melon baller or into larger balls using a small ice-cream scoop. Garnish with fresh mint sprigs and serve immediately.

frozen white chocolate mousse with black pepper

2 cups whipping cream

12 ounces white chocolate, coarsely chopped

1 jar (7 ounces) marshmallow cream

1 1/2 tablespoons crème de cacao

2 teaspoons vanilla extract

2 teaspoons very coarsely ground black peppercorns

Mint sprigs, for garnish

➤ You may serve this decadent dessert in a pool of fresh berry or dark chocolate sauce; with sliced fresh fruit; or simply garnished with fresh mint.

Instead of making an elaborate stove-top Italian-style meringue as called for in many mousse recipes, this easy-to-make dessert uses convenient jarred marshmallow cream—a terrific and versatile commercial product.

HOT 3

makes 6 to 8 servings

Place 1½ cups of the whipping cream in a small bowl and beat until stiff. Refrigerate until needed.

In the top of a double boiler, heat the remaining ½ cup whipping cream with the white chocolate over moderate heat, stirring frequently, just until the chocolate has melted. Remove from the heat and transfer to a large bowl. Add the marshmallow cream, crème de cacao, vanilla extract, and black pepper. Beat until thoroughly combined and very smooth. Fold in the reserved whipped cream and mix gently just until combined.

Spoon the mixture into individual 1-cup molds or into one large mold or shallow bowl. Cover surface with parchment or waxed paper, then with foil, and place in freezer until set, about 6 hours. Remove from molds by running hot water around the outside of the container. Flip over onto plates and garnish with fresh mint sprigs. Serve immediately.

dark chocolate bread pudding with black pepper

Preheat oven to 300° F. Place the bread cubes on a large baking sheet in a single layer. Toast 7 to 10 minutes or until crisp and very light brown on all sides. Remove from oven and cool to room temperature. Set aside.

In a 4-quart heavy-bottomed saucepan, combine the half-and-half, milk, and semisweet chocolate. Heat over moderately low heat for 3 to 4 minutes, stirring frequently, until the chocolate has completely melted. Mix well, remove from the heat, and cool slightly.

In a large bowl, whisk together the eggs, sugar, whiskey, vanilla extract, and salt. Add the cooled chocolate-cream mixture and mix well. Add the pepper, cinnamon, and reserved bread cubes; toss gently. Let stand at room temperature for 1 to 1½ hours, pressing the bread down into the liquid every 20 minutes to promote even saturation. Add the bittersweet chocolate and walnuts and toss gently.

Preheat oven to 350° F. Generously grease a shallow 3-quart ovenproof casserole.

Turn the bread mixture into the prepared casserole and bake on the middle rack of the oven 15 minutes. Reduce oven temperature to 325° F. and bake 25 to 30 minutes, or until the center jiggles slightly when shaken. Remove from the oven and let stand 5 to 10 minutes before serving.

> Bread pudding will have new appeal once you sample this unique and delectable rendition. Although it's pleasing as is, you may gild the lily by drizzling the warm pudding with crème fraîche or vanilla yogurt, or by garnishing it with dollops of whipped cream or coffee ice cream.

HOT 2

makes 6 to 8 servings

1 baguette (8 ounces), halved lengthwise and cut into 1-inch cubes (about 5 cups cubed)

1½ cups half-and-half

1½ cups whole milk

4 ounces semisweet chocolate, coarsely chopped

3 large eggs

²/₃ cup sugar

¼ cup whiskey or rum

1½ teaspoons vanilla extract

Dash kosher salt

1½ tablespoons black peppercorns, very coarsely ground

1½ teaspoons ground cinnamon

4 ounces bittersweet chocolate, very coarsely chopped

³/₄ cup walnuts, very coarsely chopped

TABLE OF EQUIVALENTS

THE EXACT EQUIVALENTS IN THE FOLLOWING TABLES HAVE
BEEN ROUNDED FOR CONVENIENCE.

US/UK

OZ=OUNCE	LB=POUND
TBL=TABLESPOON	FL OZ=FLUID OUNCE
QT=QUART	

METRIC

G=GRAM

KG=KILOGRAM

MM=MILLIMETER

CM=CENTIMETER

ML=MILLILITER

L=LITER

WEIGHTS

US/UK	METRIC
1 OZ	30 G
2 OZ	60 G
3 OZ	90 G
4 OZ (¼ LB)	125 G
5 OZ (⅓ LB)	155 G
6 OZ	185 G
7 OZ	220 G
8 OZ (½ LB)	250 G
10 OZ	315 G
12 OZ (¾ LB)	375 G
14 OZ	440 G
16 OZ (1 LB)	500 G
1 ½ LB	750 G
2 LB	1 KG

OVEN TEMPERATURES

FAHRENHEIT	CELSIUS	GAS
250°	120°	½
275°	140°	1
300°	150°	2
325°	160°	3
350°	180°	4
375°	190°	5
400°	200°	6
425°	220°	7
450°	230°	8
475°	240°	9
500°	260°	10

LIQUIDS

US	Metric	UK
2 TBL	30 ML	1 FL OZ
¼ CUP	60 ML	2 FL OZ
⅓ CUP	80 ML	3 FL OZ
½ CUP	125 ML	4 FL OZ
⅔ CUP	160 ML	5 FL OZ
¾ CUP	180 ML	6 FL OZ
1 CUP	250 ML	8 FL OZ
1 ½ CUPS	375 ML	12 FL OZ
2 CUPS	500 ML	16 FL OZ
4 CUPS/1 QT	1 L	32 FL OZ

Equivalents for Commonly Used Ingredients

All-Purpose (Plain) Flour/
Dried Bread Crumbs/Chopped Nuts

¼ cup	1 oz	30 g
⅓ cup	1 ½ oz	45 g
½ cup	2 oz	60 g
¾ cup	3 oz	90 g
1 cup	4 oz	125 g
1 ½ cups	6 oz	185 g
2 cups	8 oz	250 g

Whole-Wheat (Wholemeal) Flour

3 tbl	1 oz	30 g
½ cup	2 oz	60 g
⅔ cup	3 oz	90 g
1 cup	4 oz	125 g
1 ¼ cups	5 oz	155 g
1 ⅔ cups	7 oz	210 g
1 ¾ cups	8 oz	250 g

Brown Sugar

¼ cup	1 ½ oz	45 g
½ cup	3 oz	90 g
¾ cup	4 oz	125 g
1 cup	5 ½ oz	170 g
1 ½ cups	8 oz	250 g
2 cups	10 oz	315 g

White Sugar

¼ cup	2 oz	60 g
⅓ cup	3 oz	90 g
½ cup	4 oz	125 g
¾ cup	6 oz	185 g
1 cup	8 oz	250 g
1 ½ cups	12 oz	375 g
2 cups	1 lb	500 g

Long-Grain Rice/Cornmeal

⅓ cup	2 oz	60 g
½ cup	2 ½ oz	75 g
¾ cup	4 oz	125 g
1 cup	5 oz	155 g
1 ½ cups	8 oz	250 g

Dried Beans

¼ cup	1 ½ oz	45 g
⅓ cup	2 oz	60 g
½ cup	3 oz	90 g
¾ cup	5 oz	155 g
1 cup	6 oz	185 g
1 ¼ cups	8 oz	250 g
1 ½ cups	12 oz	375 g

Grated Parmesan/Romano Cheese

¼ cup	1 oz	30 g
½ cup	2 oz	60 g
¾ cup	3 oz	90 g
1 cup	4 oz	125 g
1 ⅓ cups	5 oz	155 g
2 cups	7 oz	220 g